THE
WEALTHY
ALIEN

DOMENIC FERRARI

Copyright © 2018 Tall Man Media Publishing

Book Cover Art by Rene Magritte.

All the characters in this book are fictitious. Any resemblance to actual persons, living or dead, is purely coincidental.

> The poor is hated even of his own neighbour: but the rich hath many friends.
>
> — Prov. 14:20

> The Fortune Teller told me a lie.
>
> — Allen Toussaint

"HERE'S TO THE CRAZY ONES. THE MISFITS. THE REBELS. THE TROUBLEMAKERS. THE ROUND PEGS IN THE SQUARE HOLES. THE ONES WHO SEE THINGS DIFFERENTLY. THEY'RE NOT FOND OF RULES. AND THEY HAVE NO RESPECT FOR THE STATUS QUO. YOU CAN QUOTE THEM, DISAGREE WITH THEM, GLORIFY OR VILIFY THEM. ABOUT THE ONLY THING YOU CAN'T DO IS IGNORE THEM. BECAUSE THEY CHANGE THINGS. THEY PUSH THE HUMAN RACE FORWARD. AND WHILE SOME MAY SEE THEM AS THE CRAZY ONES, WE SEE GENIUS. BECAUSE THE PEOPLE WHO ARE CRAZY ENOUGH TO THINK THEY CAN CHANGE THE WORLD, ARE THE ONES WHO DO."

— **Rob Siltanen**

Author's Note

Venus is the second planet from the sun. It is named after the Roman goddess. As the second-brightest natural object in the night sky after the moon, Venus can cast shadows and, rarely is visible to the naked eye in broad daylight. In ancient Roman mythology, Venus was the goddess of love, fertility and victory. Her importance to Rome stems from both her role as their mythological ancestor as well as her assistance in the Roman victory against Carthage in the Second Punic War. It saw hundreds of thousands killed, some of the most lethal battles in military history, the destruction of cities, and massacres and enslavements of civilian populations and prisoners of war by both sides. Carthage lost Hispania forever and Rome firmly established her power there over large areas. Derived from Latin, today they cover half the world.

From the very start Rome had been an open city, a safe haven for outcasts, murderers and runaway slaves. Rome offered migrants a unique opportunity to become fully fledged citizens. This made Rome the largest metropolitan city of the ancient world. The Romans themselves believed they were descendants of refugees from the Middle East who had survived the Trojan War. At its height the Roman Republic encompassed the entire Mediterranean Sea as well as expanding northward to Gaul and Britain. History records the exploits of the heroes as well as the tirades of the emperors. Despite the sometimes shameful deeds of the imperial office, the empire was built on the backs of its citizens, the unsung people who lived a relatively quiet existence and who are often ignored by history. Near the end of the Roman Empire, the Senate became a town council and the country was now ruled by an army of officials personally reporting to the Emperor. Thus the ancient world centered around the concept of a free community and free citizen came to an end, the Emperor had become the Dominus, meaning "Lord", a title by which slaves address their masters. The citizen became a subject, the warrior turned into a soldier and the farmer a semi serf, an agricultural labourer bound under the feudal system to work on his lord's estate. Diocletian himself resigned himself from the post of Emperor twenty years later and went off to his estate to grow cabbages.

At this time the central government took an active interest in supporting agriculture. Producing food was the top priority of land use. Larger farms achieved an economy of scale that sustained urban life and its more specialized division of labour. Small farmers benefited from the development of local markets in towns and trade centres. Agricultural techniques such as crop rotation and selective breeding were disseminated throughout the Empire, and new crops were introduced from one province to another, such as peas and cabbage to Britannia, still a Roman province.

Despite its enormity, at the end of its lifetime Rome was plagued by relentless barbarian attacks that chipped and pecked away its borders and by the time of Romulus there was little more than Italy left. Britannia eventually claimed their land over the Germanic Angles, Jutes and Saxons pushing back many Celts and Britons to Ireland, Scotland, Wales, Cornwall and Brittany. The Duke's faded away but the Anglo-Saxons eventually formed a number of kingdoms. As with the Romans, all the land in the empire belonged to the Emperor and he would then parcel out large estates to the various: retired military men and patricians who were those wealthy families providing the empire's political and religious leadership.

In Roman culture, it was common for a patron (a wealthy Roman citizen) to automatically retain his freed slaves in a dependent relationship, known as patronage. This required the slave to accompany his patron to war and protect him if the latter so wished, to accompany him to court as a vocal supporter and, if the patron held public office, to act as his assistant and to accompany him on representational events in public. This form of relationship between the rich-and-the-poor was increasingly adopted in rural areas, because the Roman "nomenklatura" increasingly saw their vast estates as their refuge and also as economically important pillars.

During the latter years with Germanic kingdoms on Roman soil, it was common for all the land to belong to the king. Only he could distribute land to his subjects.

These subjects were usually family members, warriors who had performed outstanding feats, and noblemen. The land did not become property of the subject but remained with the king. On the death of the king, the land was returned to the new king. Over time, a practice developed that the person deeded with the land, together with his family, became the beneficiaries and remained permanently bound to it.

The Roman patron-client relationship and the early clan-based feudal relationship in the Germanic kingdoms merged during the early Middle Ages into the feudal law, or Lehnsrecht, a legal and social set of relationships, which effectively formed a pyramid with the king at the top. The remnants of feudal system, rendering itself as early as the Western Roman Empire fall in 476 C.E., still exists today as an all-encompassing social hierarchy, a political system and economic system of both structure and harmony.

1
Woodpeckers On Venus

Brunswick Farm, appropriately known as Smitty's Farm, is located in Brunswick County, New Brunswick. The owner and resident, Mr. Elliot Archibald Smitty, belongs to a long line of wealthy landowners who were smart enough to build farms. Grandpa Gerald Fitzgerald Smitty or *Old Smitty* named after his own grandpa was the smartest of the bunch with an eagle eye for detail. He graduated from Oxford and came to Canada before the first World War. Bought into the Toronto Maple Leafs when they were still the Toronto St. Pat's and made a ton of money when Maple Leaf Gardens came along. Old Smitty journeyed out east and did the most practical and honest thing a man in his financial disposition: he lived on the land and not off the land.

"You can't run a farm today without money just as you can't build a hockey arena on Lego bricks." Mr. Smitty liked to jab me with a few of his philosophical trepidations now and again. "You can't make money running a farm either, sorry to say."

I agreed. For thousands of years the only reason wealthy land owners bought land and built farmhouses on them was so they could live life under a tax shelter. While very few farmers succeed financially, wealthy landowners have learned, or have always known, how to lose at farming and still get away with a profit. Rather than working the land, they work the tax laws. In detail, it's complicated. In concept, it's brilliant and simple: Lose money in farming and write those losses off against non-farm income. Wealthy landowners understand that it pays to be thorough and recognize where they can gain tax breaks on farmland while maintaining things that are going to retain relative value and offer an asset class from the standpoint of its created value or production.

Mr. Smitty would often say: "People out there are talking about investing in gold and precious metals but include some hogwash, call it 'land lending' and what you are basically doing is leasing your untaxed land out to an operator who will generate the income operating the property while you retain ownership. It really is no different than any other form of rental property where folks are looking to purchase five-acre pieces for half its worth just so they can run an organic farming operation. It makes no sense."

He was right. The Herd wants a position in the world, sex, intellectual mastery, creativity but had been to inept to get them. They had therefore fashioned a hypocritical creed denouncing what they wanted but were too weak to fight for – while praising what they did not want but happened to have.

"Hold a unifying project in Life," Mr. Smitty read from *How To Become Rich In A Far Away Galaxy*. Note in *Chapter 1, Verse 66*:

"Be a man of great creativity. Think like a Woodpecker. Buy trees, buy land, buy nature."

Smitty's Farm lies on three hundred acres and consists of eleven farmhouses, eight barns, four horse stables, three swimming pools, a man-made pond, two mini-golf courses, an outdoor hockey rink and a ten thousand sq. ft. mansion owned by Mr. Smitty and his wife, Mrs. Smitty. Down from the stone entranceway is farmhouse Number *1* and *2* which belong to Mr. Smitty's son and daughter, Henry and Sarah. Number *3* and *4* belong to the Doyle's and the Doyle's youngest son who lives on the farm and works for Mr. Smitty's mum. Mum lives on the east end of the farm near the pond in a converted beach house I call Number *5*. The horse trainer, housekeeper and chauffeur have Number *6*, *7* and *8* which are much smaller homes: one bedroom flats built on top of barns. Number *9* belongs to Mr. Smitty's stepsister, Josephine, and Number *10* to Mr. Smitty's stepbrother Kurt and his wife Stella. The last farmhouse across a deserted tennis court in which Mother Nature had her way is mine: Number *11*.

We don't have to worry about anybody mistaking Smitty's Farm for a plantation. We don't grow crops here and most folks in the area know Mr. Smitty as "the hospital guy" with a portfolio the size of Vermont. Smitty is the Smith in Smith & Olster Care and Canada's oldest and largest medical assistance provider in the country. Forbes reported Smith & Olster Care's net worth up and around fifty million. Some of the hands think it's a hundred million. I think it's closer to two and three hundred.

We live rent-free in a three bedroom farmhouse. The kitchen architect Hassel-Moore fixed it so the missus can see out the window while she's drying the dishes. There's a stainless steel refrigerator and convection (not conventional) natural gas oven with an emergency button in case of fire. There's an oak table in the dining area with a matching hutch packed with Royal Doulton dolls and figurines. A two-story TV Room was added three years ago which consists of two cushy L-couches, a programmable lazy chair with remote, a HI-FI stereo, my wife's sewing machine and a 65-inch 4K LED TV handpicked and paid for by the Smitty's. There's a den with an antique rotary dial telephone and all my wife's Harlequin paperbacks, a guest room for those rare times my wife's side of the family are in town and a mud room with both a ski rack and locked rifle cabinet. My girls sleep upstairs because they like to be on the same floor as us but I'm sure Becky will decide to take up the guest room downstairs one day, maybe in a couple of years when she graduates high school and starts to call me by my first name. Becky's three years older than Charlotte. They sleep next to our room, the master bedroom. I set them up in bunk beds because it makes common sense. I'm all about common sense as you will soon see. My wife, Shelley, likes that the girls have bunk beds. It keeps them cozy and close to us, she says.

    I've been on Smitty's Farm for fifteen years and I don't plan on leaving anytime soon. I'd be an idiot to move. Living on a farm owned by rich folk is like sitting on a nest of golden eggs. You really can't appreciate that until you spend a couple of months here. No matter in summer or winter you just have to be here for a couple of months. I should say a couple of things about what I do here on Smitty's Farm but I'll get into that soon enough.

I think for now it's important to understand what sets the Smitty family apart.

The Smitty family is primarily a banking family. Much of the wealth has been locked up in the notable family trust going back four generations. Management of this fortune today rests with professional money managers who oversee the principal holding company, Smith Financial Services, which controls all the family's investments. The combined personal and social connections of the various family members are vast, both in Canada and throughout the world, including the most powerful politicians, royalty, public figures and chief businessmen. It's not easy to put my finger on it but I think it's fair to say that the Smitty fortune runs somewhere in the neighbourhood of half-a-billion if you count up all the assets and trust funds.

Let me take you through Smitty's mansion on the estate or what I like to call Smitty's Roman Palace.

Okay, so you open this gigantic wooden door made from solid oak that belongs more in a Roman cathedral than a multi-million dollar converted farmhouse. I don't really use this door unless its Christmas time and then the family and I walk through the front to greet the entire Smitty family. Normally I steer my way through the side door to get in. For fun let's go through the front.

There's a huge Mahogany wardrobe closet to your left that looks antique. I don't know who owned it before the Smitty's but it looks handmade and worth a pile of money. Everything in this house looks like it's worth a pile of money. The marble table in the front room looks like it once belonged to Caesar. The cabinet in the front living room probably belonged to a Prince. Ever watch those travelling auctions with all those

English folk with stuff that's worth thousands of dollars and whose family have claimed ownership for hundreds of years? Everything here looks like it belongs in an auction. To your right is the dining room which can sit up to twenty folks over the holidays and sometimes up to thirty-five if we set up a table in the adjoining hallway. Most of the paintings in Smitty's den are worth millions. I can't be real sure but I do remember one of the old hands telling me about a Picasso being in there and this old hand wasn't the type to fib. There's a den, a living room, a dining area and a huge kitchen with a Hammacher juicer worth 10k, a Mugnainu wood-fired pizza oven, a sub-zero Wolf freezer, a wine station, a stainless steel meat counter, hidden warming drawers and radiant-heated limestone floors topped up with a metal ceiling centrepiece with an LED illuminated Onyx countertop.

There's a twenty-five-foot Christmas tree in the adjoining family room that overlooks twelve acres of rolling countryside. Me and a couple of the other hands drive up to Kook's Tree Farm and pick a monster for five hundred bucks. It's a bugger to put up but we manage. Christmas is a big deal on the farm and I do my very best to make certain the Smitty family enjoy themselves at this special time of the year. I'm well rewarded for my efforts with a case of vintage French wine and a two week round trip family vacation. We've been to California and the Grand Canyon, Las Vegas, Aruba, Bermuda, Alaska, Disneyland twice, seen the Pyramids, Tahiti and most of Western Europe. The Smitty's are special people and go all out to make me and my family feel special too.

What else? My wife calls me a miser. I don't mind. In fact, I'm proud of it. Ever seen that movie *It's A*

Wonderful Life with Lionel Barrymore? Remember Potter? Well, I understood Potter. Still do. Potter was like my Grandpa Lance: Thrifty. Bald. Cautious. Envied. Odd. There are benefits to being odd despite what you're English teacher or therapist has ever told you.

The missus hates the fact that I'm thrifty. So does my twin brother. In fact, everybody does. Most folks who know me in Brunswick call me "Penny Pinching Casey" but that's all nonsense. What most people don't know is just over sixteen years ago when my wife gave birth to our first child and I was miserably unhappy working sixty hours a week as a software salesman for IBM, that inherent thriftiness allowed me to stumble across an AD in the paper looking for a gardener position on Smitty's Farm. I still remember the look on my wife's face when I told her the opportunity of living rent-free.

"Oh?"

Her cheeks had ballooned into two ripe plumbs.

"It's out east on a farm owned by rich folk," I said in a monotone.

"Oh."

She repeated with the preciseness of a marksmen's arrow.

"You may as well quit your job at the factory."

"That sounds alright, but can we afford to just pick up and go?"

"You don't understand, sweetheart, our employers are rich, filthy rich and they're very nice people. This is not a normal combination of character."

2

Copernicus And The Crystal Ball

The role of a Roman Empress varied. The Empress would make decisions only if the Emperor was unable to rule. This could be due to illness or being too young to make decisions. The Empress was the Emperor's most trusted ally.

As Empress, Mrs. Smitty's responsibilities range from administrative duties to household duties to social or charitable duties. In other words, the poor girl is swamped. That's where I come in. I'm like her prized servant; her Roman Empire Knight. I help her delegate all the menial day-to-day tasks, from repairing the tractor to delivering calves, haying, buying feed, caring for the cattle and horses. There are hundreds of tasks each and every day and with very few hands it requires the utmost patience and focus. Especially focus. I work more than eighteen hour days when Mrs. Smitty's friends are in town. I make certain there's enough wine and cocktails, fresh scallops, shrimp, cashews, salmon dip and among other things. I make certain the tables are clean, the balloons blown, the streamers streamed. I take care of folks who need a ride to and from the airport or train station, whatever the circumstance. Just last month I rented a bus to get forty women over to the Smitty's estate for a charity luncheon in honour of Mrs. Smitty's aunt who lost her life to lung cancer. Next month we're having twenty guests fly in for an auction to raise money for the *Smith Foundation for Heart and Liver Disease*. Keep in mind most of these folks are shelling out five to ten thousand bucks a seat so they want to be at the very least chaffered, fed and entertained.

We don't use jesters like they did in the old days behaving like clowns or magicians. Entertaining the guests usually includes a violinist or a classical guitar player. We've had lots of different singers and comedians. Neil Diamond and Jim Carrey impersonators. Sometimes we'll do crazier things like rent a hot air balloon or take a trip into the city. Mostly we try and keep the show in and very professional. Although, I will say one of the hands, Beatrice, our cook, has a son who is a terrific mime and puts on a spectacular show for everybody at our annual Christmas party.

Beatrice prefers not to live on the farm. Married for over thirty years to the same man she arrives to work every day at 5:30 a.m. to make breakfast leaving at 5:30 p.m. once supper is ready to be served. A long time ago she gave up the duties of serving supper so she could get home on time for her own family. She's worked for the Smitty's nearly twenty years and earned enough money for her son to attend medical school. Good for her. I'm proud to say I lent her a tip on GIC bills that turned out profitable. I should mention that Beatrice's cooking is fantastically delicious and healthy, what can be described as "homely organic". Many of her foods include healthy brown rice, vegetables, fish, chick peas, Bok Choy, ginger root and exotic fruit like Jamaican papaya and Japanese pear. Her main course is often served with French wine attesting to her almost fanatical approach to healthy digestive eating.

Smitty's Farm requires more caring than upkeep with two Labrador retrievers and a Dutch Husky. It's important that when the Smitty's are away the dogs are kept clean and happy. The dog sitter's name is Liza with a number of responsibilities including caring for the dogs, house sitting, serving meals and general upkeep of the main living quarters. Liza lives with the Smitty's . She's single and barely out of her twenties. She's been with us for three years now and came as a referral from a friend of Mrs. Smitty's. That's really the only way you can get onto Smitty's Farm these days is by referral. Answering to a fifty dollar newspaper AD is a lost art.

The Smitty's housekeeper is named Dora and she lives off the farm. Her hours are more part-time but Mrs. Smitty makes certain she gets enough work to sustain her and her four kids. Dora's a single mother and Mrs. Smitty is well aware of her financial situation and does everything in her power to keep Dora happy. Mrs. Smitty is no dummy. She values happiness and understands that money alone will not bring happiness. The more you help other people and make them happy, the more you will be happy. She believes this. Happiness does not come through selfishness but through selflessness. You reap what you have sown.

Most of the hired hands can be found in the Great Hall which is the main meeting and dining area and used by everyone who lives on the farm. Life with the Smitty's revolves around this room. All of the meals are served in this room. Everybody ensures the Great Hall is always clean and decorated for holidays and special occasions. I especially love this room during the Christmas season. It's where we have our annual Christmas party known among the hired hands as "Christmas on the Farm": rolling out the red carpet and welcoming the Christmas spirit, forgetting all the bad and focusing on what truly matters.

Another special place on the farm is The Brewery. We don't make our own beer but we stock plenty of it. This is another one of my favourite areas. Not so much because I enjoy the odd glass but because of the wide assortment of imported beers: Brouwerij De Koninck from Belgium, Konig Pilsner from Germany, Belhaven Scottish Ale and Harviestoun Old Engine Oil from Scotland. Mr. Smitty is a huge fan of the ales from California: Bayhawk Amber Ale, Allagash White Ale and Flying Dog Tire Biter Golden Ale. He gave me the responsibility of The Brewery after one of our hands was caught passed out over an empty keg of Austrian lager.

The Brewery is different from The Cellar where we keep our wines and spirits. I also take care of The Cellar. The Cellar takes a bit more of my time with wine being the preferred drink at meals and parties. The Smitty's are big into both domestic and imports like Cavit Pinot Grigio from Italy or a Dry Riesling from locals Glenfield Farm here in Brunswick. When it comes to hard booze Mr. Smitty prefers his gin and it don't matter if it's Bluecoat, or Bombay Dry English, Magellan or Tanqueray No. 10. As long as it's served with a squirt of tonic and a slice of lime he's good. He thought about opening his own gin distillery at one time but red tape got in the way so he didn't bother, which in a funny way is very characteristic of Mr. Smitty. I don't like to talk too harshly but "blue eyes" can be a bit of a slouch when it comes to venturing into unchartered territory. He's not very business savvy let's say. Definitely not like his grandpa who was very business savvy or what some people like to call "business lucky". During his career, Old Smitty was reported to have the fourth-largest insurance company in the country with $1.2 billion in premiums and six thousand employees countrywide. I met one of Old Smitty's employees, Susan Usman, a Brunswick resident who worked at Universal Life for twenty years and said she enjoyed working for Old Smitty because he drew the best out of her by working and thinking creatively. She described him as a "brilliant, brilliant man who pushed the boundaries of conventional thinking in everything that he did and left the world better for his passions." I'm not sure if the same could be said about Mr. Smitty who sold Universal Life for a meager forty million ten years after Old Smitty's passing.

The best thing Mr. Smitty ever did and it took a whole lot of smarts was marrying Mrs. Smitty. As the story goes Mr. Smitty had a falling out with his first wife and heard about Mrs. Smitty through a friend. He heard that she'd recently divorced and moved into a high-rise in nearby Troy County, some thirty-five miles from Brunswick.

Born to a publishing mogul Mrs. Smitty grew up on an estate in "old Cape Breton" where a staff of thirty-plus servants attended to the family's every need. I don't know too much about her upbringing but I'd heard Mrs. Smitty describe her early life as a lonely time. Her mother gave incredible parties for the upper class and while Mrs. Smitty was well cared for, her mother paid little personal attention to her daughter. Mrs. Smitty would sit, hidden from view and watch as her mother entertained the fine ladies and gentlemen of high society. As a child it was said Mrs. Smitty had a love for painting. When Mrs. Smitty grew up she moved to the big city and pursued her love for art building a reputation as a world-class auctioneer.

Luckily, Mr. Smitty acted quickly when he did and snagged Mrs. Smitty. I think they make a great couple and sometimes I have to admit I envy their relationship. I love my wife but I'm not the romantic Mr. Smitty is. Legend has it during the Smitty's courtship he'd flown in an exotic pair of llamas from West Africa when he'd heard Mrs. Smitty was crazy about them. She named them Telly and Sally. Since then Telly and Sally have produced two generations of llamas who are living contently in a custom built barn on the east side of Smitty's Farm.

I'm grateful the Smitty's hooked up when they did and knew I'd made the right decision when I accepted the job back in '98. We took a real liking to each other right from the start and like most lasting relationships it's always come easy. And that's something I've learned over the years. As everyone tries so hard to make relationships work I think the best relationships require no work at all, but a genuine show of kindness.

In fact, I'm on my way over to see Mrs. Smitty and give thanks.

Not long ago my wife threw a big hissy fit saying that I'm always out hunting and nowhere to be found. I wasn't arguing with her. But she went on and on saying I'm selfish and that I don't think of anyone but myself. Then she says she wants me to prove her otherwise and clean the den where she says "there's more spiders than a fly colony", whatever that means. I'm trying to understand but what about her daughters, don't they have a responsibility to clean? I scraped the cobwebs out and stuff and when I tried talking to her about it she ignored me. So I told Charlotte and my wife found out and she threw another hissy fit again saying oh that I can't be trusted. I had a face to face with her and she says no frigging way. I'm like you're not giving me a chance. Then I'm super mad and I totally rant out my feelings in front of my daughters who say nothing because I think they're just used to it. Then Becky goes and tells Dora everything I said including when I said I hated her. I'm like what are you saying sweetheart? Anyway, it gets back to Mrs. Smitty and the next thing you know there's a box for me in the front of my house with a card saying something about "how important marriage is and how sometimes you have to keep your ill feelings to yourself." Inside the box there's a bouquet of long stem roses for the missus and a lambskin coat for yours truly.

It's just like Mrs. Smitty to get me out of a bind.

Mrs. Smitty is outfitted in a red-and white checkered apron when I slip in through the side entrance. The odor of pasta sauce trails behind her like a wedding gown train.

"Oh, Casey, you've come just in time," Mrs. Smitty says in a high shrill. "I'm up to my ears in chicken linguini. You wouldn't happen to know how long I should boil artichokes would you?"

"I don't have the faintest idea," I reply.

I'm always glad to see Mrs. Smitty. There's something special about her. I can't quite pin it. It might just be a chemical reaction between her and I. Synthesis reaction.

"I'm surprised in you. I thought all Scottish people knew how to prepare an artichoke; for goodness sake."

"Did you read the recipe book?" I suggest.

"When the day comes when I need a recipe book to boil an artichoke please don't hesitate to shoot me." She scampers about the room with an oversized fork in her hand. "How was your drive over to the Kook's Farm? I hope Kyle didn't talk you into buying anymore chickens."

"I didn't get a chance to see Kyle. I went hunting remember."

"Good. It's terrible how skinny those chickens of his are. Poor birds. I heard he counts the number of kernels he feeds them. He should be put away in one of those chicken asylums if you ask me."

The kitchen is astringently neat. On the stove a pot of spaghetti sauce simmers and a colander full of linguini stands steaming. A small drop-leaf table is set with a couple of mismatched plates and glasses which have animated cartoon figures dancing around the rims. I recognize one of the cartoon figures as Bugs Bunny.

"Thank you," I say.

"For what?"

"The coat."

She smiles as she finally notices I'm wearing lambskin.

"Wonderful. It fits like a glove."

Everybody on the farm thinks I'm spoiled. Maybe I am. If my being half English or half Scotch or Catholic or insanely humble ever helped me in any way in this life, it helped me getting the Smitty's to like me unconditionally.

"Sit down and I'll rustle up your favourite. Wieners and eggs?" Mrs. Smitty sets her fork down on the counter. "You make yourself comfortable and I'll have Beatrice in here in a jiffy." She takes my coat. "Oh, where did that creature go?"

I can't help but think of Mrs. Smitty as an angel.

In fact, she worked as an airline stewardess. She was twenty-two then. Single, unattached, and free to fly without a conscience, so to speak. She told me once how she had helped deliver a baby on a flight from Moscow to Paris. She laughed because they couldn't decide on the baby's name---Pascal, Pasha, Pasquale. They finally decided on Pascal once the plane landed.

"Mr. Smitty's away on business."

She uncorks a bottle of red wine and places a tall wine glass in front of me. She doesn't offer. She just pours.

I savour the taste.

"Casey, did I ever tell you about my little gathering in the sky?"

"No."

"I can remember cold mornings when we flew from Alaska to Los Angeles, and I would be all in furs because the heat went off, and I'd be bundling who I could, treating the passengers as if they were my own. Only I was freezing to death. And then this priest comes on board and he practically convinces this non-Catholic into a sermon and the next thing I know there's about six of them having a séance in the sky. I swear to you I heard the devil that night."

There's a cuckoo clock in the living room adjacent to where we sit and when it cuckoo's one o'clock it stirs the feathers off Mrs. Smitty and she unwittingly drops her glass.

"For heaven's sake," she bellows out. "I'm a nervous wreck. Do you want to know why, Casey?"

I nod dutifully.

"Mum isn't doing well. Seriously unwell. Mr. Smitty received the news last night. Something about her spleen bursting. She refuses to go to the hospital. So arrangements are being made," she says. "There's not much else to it. A couple of meetings down south with our lawyer just in case. It really is more than a necessity when you come right down to it. I find it quite cumbersome myself. But it has to be done. My goodness. Do you smell the linguini burning?"

It's a bit arrogant that Mrs. Smitty refers to her husband in the third person, but I'm used to it. I guess I've talked myself into believing it's the proper way of communicating among the upper class.

"I had Beatrice make some tenderized pork loin with Columbian string beans before Mr. Smitty flew."

All of a sudden the door blasts open, and the beasts barge in and almost smother Mrs. Smitty. Her dogs love her. She kisses each of them on the mouth.

I sit quietly.

Mixing a plate, Mrs. Smitty unravels a large helping of linguini down on three separate plates.

"They love Italian food."

Pooches, the Lab, begins to rummage through her sister's plate when Mrs. Smitty smacks her on the behind.

"You leave Francie's plate alone. Silly girl," Mrs. Smitty says. "If there's one thing I can't stand in a girl is that selfishness quality. Boy! That really irks me."

When the dogs are finished Dora takes the responsibility of cleaning up after them. "Did you want them out for the afternoon, Mrs. Smitty?"

"Yes, my dear," Mrs. Smitty says. "Please make sure they don't run too much."

Mrs. Smitty looks over to me with a playful sneer.

"Frodo was literally sick as a dog from running all afternoon the day before last."

I smile and finish my glass.

"Have you had Kurt's wine? I think converting that old barn into a winery was an ingenious idea."

"I haven't."

"You must go see him. Take Alfred with you."

Mrs. Smitty refills my glass.

"Oh, there you are, Beatrice, thank god! Have you seen Alfred?"

Beatrice appears with a crate in her grasp.

"No. I had to get more apple cider vinegar from The Cellar. Is everything alright?"

"Fine, dear."

Mrs. Smitty starts moving about the kitchen again having moved from a scamper to a slumber. She isn't a big woman but she can hold her wine. It wouldn't be fair to call her overweight standing straight and tall as she does. Kinda like how a female giraffe holds her posture.

"Casey, is it true you talk to your cows?"

I smile but I don't say a word. Part of me wants to play the game Hide and Don't Tell.

"It's alright by me," she says. "Some of the girls overheard you calling one of them Patsy and the other George. Personally, I think it's not strange at all. I talk to my plants all the time and named my beloved tulips Delilah after my mother." She peers over to Beatrice. "Do you talk to your cats, love?"

Beatrice is caught off guard but does her best to accommodate Mrs. Smitty. She adjusts her blouse and takes an extra pause to review her thoughts and dutifully replies: "I believe I do."

"See."

I laugh, like a deaf guy reading the lips of a drunken woman. Mrs. Smitty asks me, "Who are Patsy and George?"

I'm a bit embarrassed to answer Mrs. Smitty's question to be quite honest and I'm sure she sensed my discomfort. "Oh, it bothers you. Forget it. I understand. It's personal."

Eventually I take a more serious side in reminding Mrs. Smitty about my twin brother visiting. I thought it would be good for him to get away to the country, I explain. He's under great strain having just lost his business and I'd like him to have a taste for farm life and perhaps even move down.

"Is that what's been troubling you? You're stressed for your brother? I was just saying to Mr. Smitty, I don't think Casey is unhappy in his marriage."

The phone rings and Beatrice answers it.

Mrs. Smitty goes on saying that my concerns for my twin are noble but very immature. She refers to me as Brunswick's Robin Hood and adds jokingly with a rather embarrassed air that people who put other people before them are tragic figures.

Beatrice hangs up the phone.

"That was Becky, Casey."

"Becky?"

"She told me to tell you that your TV isn't working and when you have a minute to drop by and have a look at it. She said she tried moving the antenna around but it didn't work like the last time and it's very important that she catch the last episode of The Voice because it's semifinal night."

"Thanks, Beatrice."

Mrs. Smitty raises a brow. "The TV giving you problems, Casey?"

"It's fine," I say.

"It can't be fine if your Becky says it isn't." Mrs. Smitty looks at me square in the eyes when she goes on. "Your Becky is growing into a beautiful young woman. She needs her television."

Mrs. Smitty gets up from her stool and adds that life is too short to sit, especially when one is a little drunk. "Beatrice, be sure Casey finishes his plate," she ends with a hiccup. "I'm going for a nap. I hate afternoons. Goodnight, love."

3
Two Jupiters

Have a look at last month's Ad in the Sun. I put it there myself: "We're in Brunswick, Smitty's Farm, on the lookout for a gardener. Live rent-free, plus salary." Know how many responses I got with this Ad? Zero, nil, notta. That's the problem with most folk. They just don't see a great offer when it's staring them square in the face. Can you blame folks? Not really. I mean who believes the paper anymore? My twin brother's a great example. His name's Ted. Like Ted Turner. Unlike Ted Turner, my Teddy never reads the paper and lives miserably in debt. He's a recluse when it comes to following the Financial Post and has never had a care in the world for social or monetary aptitude. He's got a wife and two boys and lives in the suburbs, where I came from, a town called Beeton, 50km north of Toronto, in a cute little subdivision named "Stoned Haven". I love them to death.

Teddy and I attended university together. The joke's always been that he graduated with a degree and got stupid. I dropped out and got smart. Teddy wanted to make a million bucks the fast way. Who didn't in university? Anyway, telephone conversation hasn't changed much between the old boy and I.

"I told you a million times you can't make a million bucks selling computers."

"Sure, I can," Teddy grovelled. He grovels a lot.

"No, you can't," I insisted. "And you want to know why?"

"Why?"

"Because unless you own the patent you'll end up selling your soul and making somebody else rich."

"Selling my soul?"

"Yup."

He went quiet then. "Teddy?"

"Yeah."

"You still there?"

"Yeah."

"Look, I don't want you to feel sore but it's time you set yourself straight. For your kid's sake. Pack your bags and come and see me."

"See you about what?"

"You just come out here and see me and I'll put you straight once and for all."

Straight in my head meant putting his financial chaos in order. Do you want to hear what he said when I asked him what he'd planned to do with eliminating debt?

"I'll get a loan."

"A loan for what?" I asked.

"To pay my loan."

"You're getting a second loan to pay for your first loan?"

"Yeah."

"What happens when you can't pay your second loan?"

"I'll get a third loan," he said.

"You'll get a third loan so you can pay the second loan that you got to pay the first loan?"

"Yeah."

His solution read like an old nursery rhyme:

'I knew an old lady who swallowed a bird. How absurd, to swallow a bird. She swallowed a bird to catch the spider that wiggled and jiggled and tickled inside her... she swallowed the spider to catch the fly but I don't know why she swallowed the fly I guess she'll die.'

"You see, Teddy, everything you've done is absolutely counter-productive," I said, "It's like trying to scale a pyramid wall. You are the cause of all your debt. You are solely responsible with the unaided burden of time. Time that finally caught up to you. It's okay. It happens to everyone. Don't worry about anything. Taking responsibility is hard. It means you have to give up the victim role. But it's the only way you can empower yourself and take charge of your life. I'll put you straight, little brother. You come see me in Brunswick and all your problems will be solved. Are you with me?"

It's about a twenty-five hour drive from Beeton to Brunswick, heading east to the Atlantic Ocean. I told Teddy he didn't need to worry about living expenses as long as he stayed with me.

"There's plenty of room on the floor for you and the missus," I said.

Needless to say, my twin fought it, saying something about high gas prices. I didn't argue with him. I drive a vintage 1972 Buick Skylark. She's been with me for twelve years and hardly given me a hiccup. But then I don't take her out much. I keep Little Rhonda who I named after a Beach Boys classic chained to a fence in case anyone wants to take her. She's blue with an original horn, mag rims and saddled with a soft-top. I bought her at an auction in town around the time Charlotte was born.

I told my brother the only way to travel is by Greyhound.

"You can't beat it," I said. "For four you're looking at ninety-nine bucks. That's a steal anyway you look at it."

"Ninety-nine bucks?"

"All in," I said. "It's a family special run every third week of September."

For ninety-nine bucks he agreed to come and see me.

"Great," I said. "I'll see you soon." Click.

I knew Teddy was in trouble or I wouldn't have been so direct. Then if I had myself down half-a-million I'd want someone to help me up. It's probably closer to a million now – two mortgages on the house and cottage, ten credit cards (including the wife's), an overdue line of credit, a boat loan and a hundred other miscellaneous expenses: gasoline for the van, cottage repairs, War Amp donations, manicures, wedding gifts, health club memberships, hockey sticks, golf clubs, flowers, Girl Guide cookies, you know the list. He's got a hundred, maybe a thousand, hungry mice in his pocket scratching for a piece of cheese.

No fault to him. Teddy was the captain of his football team. An A+ Student. Voted most likely to succeed. But something went wrong. He lost control. I'm not sure if his job with a Fortune 500 company had anything to do with it. I can only speculate. The sign of unhappiness is there. He recently discovered, with the help of a therapist, that he's severely depressed and suffers social anxiety. He realized that he'd been holding in all of his emotional baggage for years and that all at once something triggered these feelings to surface causing what seems like a nervous breakdown in his life. He was always the gentle giant that owned the room without having to do much. He was always outgoing, a great conversationalist and funny. Over the last few years I noticed a gloomier tone in his voice and a drop of motivation. We haven't talked much about medication but I'm sure he's on something with his constant fits of rage and hopelessness. I'm sure some doctor has suggested Percocet or Haldol or whatever they're stacking the shelf with these days. I want to discuss his depression and learn what's going on, but he literally starts to have what seems to me like panic attacks every time I get things going. Then the telephone is no place to talk of such personal matters. I want to help him and I'm trying my best to balance his illness and his financial strain but let me tell you, it's no easy task. I know his money matters have taken a nose dive because of his low self-esteem and he probably doesn't realize that money or a lack of it doesn't determine who he is. His worth as a person has nothing to do with how much money he has. Once he's made aware of this and understands that money is not an indication of self-worth, he'll be able to tear down the psychological barriers that are keeping him from wisely handling the money he once had. Teddy's low self-esteem is keeping him from being emotionally sound. How do I know this? We're twins. Although, it's funny to me that Teddy should look exactly like me and act exactly the opposite. We're both tall and thin as twigs. Like dad, we both have dark-brown hair that kicks out in front and a slight cowlick in the back. We've got the same coloured eyes as dad too – green. Teddy looks a lot more like mom did at the end of her life. He wouldn't be so wrinkled if he stopped smoking. Like mom, he never understood anything that required discipline. He's a worrier. Mom was a worrier. I've never worried about anything. Like my dad.

My dad always said: "Success and happiness starts with a good night sleep. "If you're too busy to get a little shut eye you're probably too tired to think and realize nobody on this planet ever worked an honest shift on three and a half hours of sleep." He's right. Try working an eight hour day with your eyes closed.

Just so you know my twin and I had a very happy childhood. We're lucky, we had very loving parents. My dad worked hard as a bricklayer and my mom's lazy, I mean, she was a housewife. Kidding, mom!

We were given a fair allowance each week, two tickets to the matinee every Saturday afternoon, no big hang ups with low grades, use of the car, tolerable curfews. I never made my bed or lifted a frying pan. The laundry was always done and I don't ever remember making breakfast or ironing my shirts. Again, thanks mom! Dad was different. He made us work for our allowance (mowing the lawn, shovelling snow off the walkway) although I will say if we ever came up short he made certain we had all the toys: GI-Joe with the Kung-Fu grip, skateboards, ping pong table, hockey sticks, Atari.

At eleven my life changed forever when my dad bought my brother and I our first game console. I'll never forget it.

"How much is Atari?" Dad said to the store clerk in an over-surprised, repetitive voice. "How much?!"

We were at Towers (that's the Canadian version of Target back in the seventies). I can still see the clerk's outfit. He was wearing a brown shirt and yellow tie. I couldn't help but laugh. There just wasn't any common sense in wearing a brown shirt with a yellow tie.

"That's two hundred and sixty-nine dollars, sir?"

I remember thinking, Wow! Two hundred a sixty-nine bucks is a lot of frigging money. Well over my dad's weekly salary.

"How will you be paying, sir?"

It occurred to me then that this Atari purchase was the biggest ticket item dad had ever bought for us.

"Master Card."

It was then that I said: "No, dad. We don't really need Atari."

I remember the horrible stare from my brother, but I persisted. "No, really, dad."

"It's alright, Casey."

"Dad?"

"Would you like that in a bag, sir?"

"You're embarrassing me, Casey."

I shut my mouth then. I never liked to upset my brother. I've got a soft place for my Teddy. Always have. Maybe because he's my twin or maybe because I know I'm smarter than him. I'd behaved sympathetically toward my dad and my brother resented that. Then I resented the fact that my dad had owed more money than he had. That said, in another place and another time you would have known how reckless the MacDonald's lived, ignoring basic monetary rules and realizing much, much too late that borrowed money wasn't salvation. We had been on three occasions users of the community food bank. This is true. That my dad resented his childhood living in the projects with six sisters and carrying no luxuries and then being forced out of school at sixteen and into a bricklayer apprenticeship. He had been seeking salvation early on. Foolishly he spent all his earnings and then some living with an attitude of Laugh Now, Cry Later. In no time he found my mother and carried on living the disjointed Canadian Dream piggybacking their neighbours below, working double bubbles and holidays, travelling down south and burning every bit of their accumulated earnings on America's answer to the All-Inclusive Getaway. A few years later my dad knocked my mother up and had me and my brother and moved into a three thousand square-foot house in Beeton. Here's an online definition: "Beeton is an elegant, large suburban community with a population over eighty thousand. It was once a farming town before being amalgamated with nearby communities."

I always thought it should have read:

"Many years ago, not many, maybe thirty, there was a small farming town called Beeton with a quaint town hall and two access highways which served as a thruway to more busier industrial towns. One day some smart real estate developer came along and proclaimed:

"This is our land." So they stayed put and built.

And, guess what? People came... thousands of them. They couldn't build fast enough. Even poor folk like my folks with no down payment could buy in Beeton. Life was one big assembly line and my folks rode the conveyor belt of luxury. Beeton was famous for offering an opportunity to live in a grandiose sized home without a reliable income. Mom and dad mortgaged their lives, had Teddy and I, barbecued and drank with our neighbours next door for the next two decades. We lived like Kings and Queens, my brother and I like Princes. We went away for two weeks every year, leased a brand new car every three years, bought a new refrigerator and stove every four. The swimming pool and hot tub built and installed when I turned thirteen, the personal workout room and sauna at fourteen, the home theatre at fifteen, my Mazda Miata and my brother's Mustang at sixteen, a Caribbean cruise at seventeen, my mom's anniversary diamond bracelet at eighteen, the funeral...

At twenty years old I buried my dad with dignity while he left us owing over two hundred and seventy-five thousand dollars. Mom met up with him one year later after she claimed bankruptcy.

I thought about those credit lines and credit cards for a long time after my folks passed away. I thought about how the Devil raised his mighty sword over my mom and dad and would one day make an example out of me as the Angel of Death did over every first born over two thousand years ago.

I met and married my wife at twenty-three years old and bought a half-a-million dollar house on a combined income of sixty-five thousand, travelled across Europe on our honeymoon. At twenty-four I bought a Nissan GT, a Range Rover for my wife six months later. Installed a kidney-shaped swimming pool at twenty-five, added the sauna, hot tub and big screen TV at twenty-six, the Alaskan cruise at twenty-seven, my wife's fifth anniversary sapphire earrings at twenty-eight, my first child came along at twenty-nine... so did the realization that I owned eight credit cards and a credit line totalling three hundred and fifty thousand. I was barely thirty and I'd already surpassed my own parent's demise.

It took to filing for bankruptcy to understand that I'd had no right as a poor man living the life of a rich man. I had no right to misinterpret what had existed for thousands of years; that to be indebted was to be poor. There have always been two classes of people and only two: wealthy and poor. And I'd forgotten some key important facts. Wealthy people don't have to work. Poor people have to work. Poor people have to work or they have no money. Wealthy people earn money when they don't work. Poor people own a mortgage. Wealthy people own a house. Poor people borrow money. Wealthy people lend money and drive expensive cars. Poor people drive expensive cars and get drunk every weekend and go back to work on Monday. Wealthy people get drunk and take Monday's off.

It took me a failed suicide attempt to finally understand.

That my entire outlook on life had to change. It was 1998. I was thirty-one years old working as an up and coming executive at IBM. I just finished a shift. I'm tired and my tally sheet clocks me in at over four hundred and fifty-eight calls. I leave the office speaking briefly with my wife on my Motorola cellular phone and check into a Super 8 motel room where I unsuccessfully hang myself.

I'd told my wife I loved her and that I was going to hang myself and she didn't believe me until I showed up with eleven stitches on my forehead later that night. I told her that I'd gone ahead with the hanging but the shower rod busted and I smacked my forehead on the base of the toilet. I said to her I'd gotten lucky.

"Yes," she said. "Luckily, you're stupid."

I looked at her and smiled.

In the morning I sat at my kitchen table and I called in sick to work and spent the next eight hours going over my incompetence's. I couldn't be so stupid to have attempted to kill myself and failed, I thought. I'd gone to the full extent of planning my suicide and had all the financials worked out. I had the nylon rope, a fifth of bourbon, my favorite CD. The appropriate insurance papers were signed and sealed. There would be enough money to pay for my funeral and cremation, car loan, line of credit, credit cards, education fund for my daughter. After all said and paid the girls would be up a half a million bucks. I'd done the math. I was organized. YES!!! FINALLY THE PAIN of financial burden would be over. No more harassing phone calls, NO MORE SLEEPLESS NIGHTS!! My girls would now be happy and half way to a million.

Then how did I fail? How could have I been so ignorant and stupid?

I'd thought about a shotgun, but I'd read Jean Maurice Claude's book on the afterlife entitled *What To Expect When You Die* and how he said hangings were much more rewarding than a self-inflicting gun wound, so I figured, you know, better not take the chance in case I'm called in front of the committee.

I remember the day of, just before arriving to the motel. I'd spent the entire night tightening the noose while listening to Iron Butterfly. I wanted everything perfect. I wanted to feel good when I went. I figured my chances of going to a heaven like place were good thus far, Hell would be a considerable far second acknowledging all that I'd sacrificed in the last twenty odd years. I went to depths in understanding death and the afterlife and the role I would play. Perhaps I would be granted Angel status. Jean Maurice Claude said that there were many dads in positions of guardianship available.

I said goodbye to many of my friends. I ate my last meal: steak and eggs. I wrote a letter to my daughter telling her how much I loved her. I wrote a letter to my wife telling her how sorry I was. I wrote a letter to my brother saying that I would miss him but that I wasn't expecting him for another fifty years. I ended with, "I'll buy you a *Canadian*." I wrote a letter to the world, something like... It may be hard for you younger kids to understand but if you haven't been to a head doctor... don't bother. Go see your bank manager.

Then I did it. I tied the noose around my neck... then it didn't happen! As I sat there at my kitchen table, in deep thought, I turned to the last page of the paper looking for the funnies when I saw something from the corner of my eye that ignited a fire. No, I didn't see THE ALMIGHTY AND POWERFUL. I saw the AD to Smitty's Farm and I called the Smitty's using my last dime.

"Sounds like you're ready for a new chapter in your life," I remember feeling how at ease Mr. Smitty had made me. "We need fellas like you who have something to prove."

"I hope I'm not coming across desperate, Mr. Smitty," I replied.

"Give it a rest my boy," he said. "Keep in mind your talking to an old dog. I've heard it all." He went on with a little gasp and chuckle. "There's nothing to fear but fear itself. The fact that you picked up the phone was the first step in the right direction. It's your lucky day. You're among friends now."

"How can you tell, sir?"

"Like I said, my boy. I've been around. I know an honest man when I hear one. Besides, I took the liberty to talk with your wife. She vouched for you."

4
Blue Mathematics

My grandpa's name was Lance. I'm not sure why he encouraged my dad to name me Casey. He had such a proper name. Lance belongs to Princes and Kings. Casey sounds like a dog's name. Like Butch. Grandpa wore glasses all his life. You've seen them round specs, James Joyce wore them. Lennon wore them. Freud too. Grandpa would have been ninety this year. Probably would have still been working. He worked as a laborer for nearly forty years. Built most of the roads I drove on for a good part of my youth. In a sense his legacy lives on those paved roads. He was a common sense man. He said time-tables were enough math for anybody. Nobody ever got rich on Algebra.

 A lot of people called my grandpa a miser but I never paid much attention. See, like millions of folks back in the day my Grandpa came from poverty. A dime was a meal. A wool sock was as good as an overcoat. Ketchup was gravy. There was no such thing as TV or satellite communication. Moms owned a Singer sewing machine with a foot pedal and you went to bed after supper.

The first MacDonald's settled in Canada in the early part of the 19th Century, in nearby Nova Scotia. The family name MacDonald comes from the name MacDhomhnuill. Mac means "son" and Dhomhaill means "of Domhnall" or "of the world". I've always been proud to have the same surname as our first Prime Minister of Canada, Sir John A. MacDonald.

Grandpa was born in Glasgow, Scotland and grew up supporting Rangers Football Club. He played hooky by the River Kelvin and married his childhood sweetheart in his late teens.

He and my grams came over with his six daughters and my dad sometime after the A-bomb dropped on Hiroshima. They settled in the city. My grandpa set the family up in a war home. You've seen them. Boxy. One level. No garage. One entrance. Two bedrooms. A living room large enough for one couch. A small kitchen with a tiny refrigerator. One bath. The girls slept in the only room with a lock while Grandpa and my dad slept on the couch in the living room. Grandpa was pretty keen on giving privacy to the girls.

They ate from the garden in the summer and salvaged leftovers the rest of the year. A lot of potatoes and corn. You know the recipes: Potato and Corn Casserole, Sweet Potato and Corn Chowder and Potato and Corn Cake.

Why potatoes and corn? Here's a quick history lesson: A long time ago potatoes and corn were important to Europe in that they diversified the food supply for many impoverished folks. Although corn is a very North American crop, its uses in Europe were widespread, many till today. An example of an undiversified crop was the French Revolution where peasants relied on the wheat and flour to make bread. Once these not so resilient crops were destroyed by harsh cold, the peasants began to starve and could not afford to buy into the dwindling food supply. Potatoes grow underneath the ground and cannot be burned or easily destroyed by climate. However, many used the crop so extensively that it replaced wheat as main diet. The Great Potato famine in Ireland was caused by a mildew that caused the potato to mold and crumble. Millions starved and were forced to flee the land of hunger. Luckily, everything turned out good at the end and we're still eating corn and potatoes today because potatoes and corn carry a high source of starch and starch is the most important carbohydrate in the human diet.

Potatoes have gotten such a bad rap over the past twenty years as little more than a waist-thickening waste of calories. But guess what? Amazing new research puts potatoes squarely at the center of the latest weight-loss buzz, along with other unfairly maligned carbohydrates such as corn and rice.

The reason: All these foods contain resistant starch, a unique kind of fiber you'll be hearing a lot more about. Don't believe me. Here's one Ad taken out of the Brunswick Tribune: *Resistant starch: The new power nutrient!*

Let me keep it simple. Why are potatoes good for us? Because they fill our tummy's when we are hungry. True. Why else? Because they're cheap! And money don't grow on trees. If they did we'd all have a money tree, right?

I remember the first time I asked my grandpa about growing a money tree like Jack in *Jack and the Beanstalk* and he laughed:

"You remember what happened to that poor giant?"

"He fell to the ground," I said.

"He flattened Jack's house with mum in it."

I don't remember that part of the story, I told my gramps. We later talked and about how grownups had to pay taxes and I told him I'd heard something on TV about fixing numbers so my dad didn't have to pay the tax man.

"What's fixing?" my grandpa said.

"Fixing's like counting cards."

"Counting cards?"

"Sort like seeing the future, grandpa."

"Betting on the future?" he said with a wrinkled brow. "I'd be careful what you want to see if I were you".

He went on talking about Cousin Fred. "Americans have Uncle Sam, Casey. We Canucks have Cousin Fred. You can fool Cousin Fred if you want but just don't think you're fooling him, you know what I mean?"

"Huh?"

"Don't make Cousin Fred your enemy. Make him your associate. Your friend. Try and understand him. Remember, Cousin Fred will leave your accrued wealth alone. Like every good communist, Cousin Fred only wants his share."

What I think my grandpa was trying to say was, there's a misconception out there by most folks when it comes to the topic of paying taxes. Too often we put the blame on something we've already been taught to dislike. I typed in the word "Taxman" online and guess what I found:

"Not afraid of the taxman? You should be."

Here's another entry right off the first page on Google search:

"Beat the Taxman With Tax-Free Income: Jump start your wealth-building efforts by increasing your tax-free income."

Sounds like a lynching if you ask me.

The truth is it's tough to get ahead financially whenever the taxman gets a big, double-digit percentage of each dime you earn. You can minimize the impact that Cousin Fred and Uncle Sam has on your finances by fixing him in the long run. Fixing? What's fixing? Is that slang for fooling or distorting. Remember folks, especially you folks with little ones. Don't believe everything you hear or read.

So why pay taxes? Because we have to. Christ's disciples had to.

See, there is a Tax Man Misconception. He's actually a nice guy. Okay, that might be hard to digest so let's go back and ask ourselves: what are the benefits of paying tax? Well, you pay taxes so other people can sit around on their fat behinds all day collecting welfare cheques while you work your own off. Seriously though - schools, emergency services (fire, ambulance, police), mail service, road construction, public buildings, parks, museums, welfare if you ever need it.

Big deal, right?

Consider something my grandpa told me:

"Casey, stop blaming the government."

In an effort to help those who suffer from the delusion that the government is filled with nothing but demonic parasites or feel they pay too much in taxes or that all of their taxes are wasted, I thought I'd create a list of benefits to kill any doubt over such depraved and selfish thoughts. If you feel the Taxman must die then please: Learn to ride a horse you may find it easier than driving your Hyundai Genesis on unpaved roads. Rip up your OHIP card. Buy an extra plunger in case your toilet backs onto your living room carpet. Your public utility offices are now 7-Elevens. Your highest discretionary expense is garbage disposal.

Buy a gun and get used to fending for yourself when travelling salesmen come knocking at your door. Look in the dictionary under extortion victim because that'll be you. Don't look too worried when Mental Health Club of America calls and asks you for membership.

Get used to buying a cob of corn for ten bucks. You thought gas was expensive wait'll you get your next cellular phone bill. Plan on homeschooling. Say goodbye to the Toronto Maple Leafs unless you want to pay for Leaf TV. Worried about losing your job? You should be.

Plan to retire in your mom's basement. Remember buying milk in a glass jug. Plan on being a single parent. Don't bother exercising for the 5KM run this year. Careful riding public transit. Don't forget your Debit Card on your next physical? In case of flooding keep a spare bathtub in the garage. Turn the channel to the Travel Show and plan your next vacation just down the road. Don't plan on visiting Mars anytime soon.

Better run when crossing the road. Sleep with your eyes open. Baseball bats are not for baseball anymore. Don't bother studying for exams. Tell your kids you used to be able to read for free at the local public library. Don't plan on owning a business. Plan on converting your wine cellar into an economy sized bomb shelter. 35% of your income will be spent on batteries. Remember what lamb tastes like. Plan on burying your loved-ones in an Easy-To-Build incinerator. Don't go hunting unless you are prepared to die in a cross-fire. Learn how to say pretty please. Get the picture.

5
The Elephant Vacuum

Some years ago I realized if I was going to be financially fearless most of the burden would have to be dissolved in discretionary income. I was probably the only guy in the whole world that didn't value the money I spent on luxury items or the ways in which I wasted money. My grandpa was a gardener and he'd be the first one to tell you that something as minimal as water shortage was no laughing matter. Think of all the water we waste with washing dishes, watering the lawn, filling up the hot tub, flushing the toilet, shaving, gargling, cooking. Now think of all the ways water can be saved: fixing faucet leaks, shorter showers, less fires.

The point is water conservation is important in everyday life. It is no different on a farm. Even Marigold Klume, the woman who wrote *500 Gallons a Day*, ever imagined that her family of four consumed up to five hundred gallons of water per day. Five hundred gallons per day? That's enough water for sixty showers a day or sixty loads in your dishwasher. I ran these numbers past the Smitty's and they nearly had a heart attack.

"Go see Homer, Casey."

For years we bought all our milk from the Griffith Farm, and just recently I heard from Alfred (you'll meet him shortly) that old J.J. "Homer" Griffith started converting his fresh water supply into bottled water reserves, investing a half million bucks to get it going. I couldn't believe it. Old Homer got water-wise! Just last year, the Griffiths, who were contently going about their rural life, mucking stalls, making garden and caring for livestock. Homer Griffith and his wife were struggling to remodel the one hundred year old farmhouse located on two acres of pristine farmland that included a fresh water ravine. They`d worked like dogs for years not realizing the potential for bottling natural spring water appropriately named after the old man himself.

"Homer's Spring Water, eh? That old bugger finally used the old noggin."

You can say the Griffith's weren't the only ones who had to loosen their creative belt to keep alive. The strength of the US Dollar and increased taxes combined with low prices for many agriculture products put a strain on the Canadian market so other families that were currently in the dairy market were now looking for wider streams, so to speak. Manufacturing bottled spring water became somewhat of a springboard to the future having the operational side of the business already in place. The old motto of "Farm Milk is Good Milk" was shelved for "Quench Your Health with Natural Spring Water".

I wanted to see the new operation for myself so I planned on Alfred and I making a stop to see Old Homer on our route which included dropping off chickens for the Donner Farm down in Minden, loading up some feed at the Hornsby Farm in nearby Truro and making our way east to Kurt's new place to pick up a couple of cases of wine for Mrs. Smitty. If we had time we'd stop at Gillian's Apple Farm for some delicious apple cider.

The Doyle farmhouse stands on a hill overlooking the east side of Smitty's pond. It was built of red and silver panels and Alfred told everyone he christened it a long way back with a bottle of Yukon Jack. It was high up, a good place from which to enjoy the view of spring sunshine over a body of water reserved for mostly Brook trout; one of the reasons why Alfred and Barb Doyle named their only daughter Brooke.

Alfred works mostly for Mr. Smitty's Mum who everyone refers to as Mum. Alfred came to Smitty's Farm back in the sixties with his wife Barb and raised sons Franklin and Patrick and daughter Brooke. Barb was a hard working hand who knew how to maintain a household. On weekends it wasn't uncommon for her to kick it into high gear when Alfred got too busy with chores or a friendly game of Twenty-One. On her days off she piddled in almost every room of her house and doted over her teaspoon collection. She painted when she had the energy and sold her prized portraits at a local flea market in town.

Having grown up in Brunswick Barb was on a first-name basis with virtually every landowner in town, many of whom knew Alfred's dad or knew close friends and relatives who worked with the old man. Gary Doyle was well respected in Brunswick and this benefited both Alfred and Barb from time to time. Barb especially. Who was driven by some of Mr. Smitty's friends all around town and knew of their private club where they rode their horses and drank vintage wine into the early hours. Barb visited the club at least once a month, it seemed, and it was not uncommon for these folks to stop her and ask about Mum. Especially as of late. Everybody knew of her weakening health. Some people said it was the Devil making a house call.

"Mum feeling okay?"

"Gotta screw loose does she?"

"Going bonkers I hear?"

"Cuckoo?"

"You don't see birds flying above, do ya?"

"Talking to wolves?"

So it was to no one's surprise that Alfred spent most of his days tending to Mum's commands.

"Alfred, you go on up to Freedman's Farm and get us some turkeys."

"Yes, mum."

"Alfred, stop by Eugene Holden's Farm and pick us some mushrooms."

"Yes, mum."

"Alfred?"

"Yes, mum."

Mum was undoubtedly the Doyle's responsibility while the rest of us took care of the Smitty's. Alfred had been common-law with Barb, surprisingly, for years and knew she had no interest in the reported common state of marriage. It was his third going and her second. She was profoundly liberated while he was perfectly illiterate. Alfred lived like those folks in Gabriel Garcia Marquez's *One Hundred Years of Solitude* – by memory. You could ask Alfred the time and he'd tell you "long hand's pretty much past the middle," which meant: Half past six. Ask him what day it was and he'd tell you Church Day. Ask him the following day and he'd tell you Work Day. The day after that was Feed Day. The one after that: Hog

Day and so on. Better off knowing "what it was for" then "what it was."

Only the morning paper was a problem, but Alfred relented to bad news and over the years learned to delegate. Anytime he was required to open the mail addressed by the Canadian government or answer to a long lost relative Barb stepped in. She paid the bills. She signed the cheques. She drove. It all worked.

"Hey, Alfred, did you hear we're getting phones? You can talk to your wife when you're out haying the fields."

"You're fooling?"

"Nope."

"How they get the cord long enough?"

"Cordless now, Alfred."

"You fooling?"

"Nope."

Alfred smiled then. He had a wicked smile mixed with a dash of both naivety and intrigue. "Can't be."

"I'm not fooling."

Alfred also had a grin about him – both unsure and deliberating. "I'm not too keen on telephones, anyways."

"You don't have a choice. We're all getting one."

"I'm still not keen on it."

Then Alfred's like those old TV sitcom characters. Literally. Wearing the same flannel blue shirt, day in and day out. His khaki pants pulled too high and tightened with a thick black leather belt. He always wears a baseball cap. No matter the team. He can't decipher logos. At seventy years old Alfred makes me look ten years my senior. Some of the female hands like Beatrice and Dora have pinpointed his youthfulness to his glowing white oversized false teeth that gives resemblance to a young

Gomer Pyle. Alfred's not aware of Gomer. Alfred's never owned a television.

Nevertheless, Alfred and Barb have raised good kids on Smitty's Farm and managed to pay for their eldest son's university education when the time came around. Brooke married young. Sixteen. And started a family the following year with Jesse Chisholm's boy who was already in medical school studying to be a vet. They moved out west about three years back. Doing well. Alfred brags about Brooke any chance he gets.

Franklin is the only kid left and at the age of forty-one is more than self-assured and financially independent. Some folks say Franklin is already a millionaire. Two times over. I believe it. As long as I've known Franklin he's held two jobs. Working twelve hour days at the feed mill and gardening Mum's rosebushes on the weekends.

Okay, so Alfred and I set off for Minden sometime around noon.

Not much to see heading east on Kirby Road with so few paved roads and plenty of cornstalk. We came to a corner gas station, Old Man Weatherly's Gas Stop, followed by a stretch of deep woodland, then open cornstalk again, and it was while passing through this cornstalk that Alfred got this idea about selling dried cornstalk. He asked me if I'd ever seen a cornstalk fire and I told him I hadn't. He said it blew a pretty intense flame and burned just as good if not better than charcoal.

"You fooling?"

"I'm not fooling," he said with a serious grin.

Alfred was always full of inventive ideas. I heard from Barb that he liked to build model airplanes in his spare time. She said he was talented. I'm not surprised. Alfred always struck me as an analytical person who paid a lot of attention to detail. You can say Alfred loved detail. He could drive you insane with detail in fact. Our entire drive he kept reiterating instructions about how he wanted me to handle the steering wheel.

"You oughta keep both hands on the wheel, Casey. No sense in using one and not the other."

I gaze up at the reservoir with black lettering written on its neck: Town Of Minden. It's big enough to quench the thirst of a Bavarian giant right out of a Grimm's fairy tale. After staring at it a moment or so, I steer down the hill and come to a wooden barrier. After driving around it I swerve around a number of orange pylons that skirt a deep rutted hole. Again we're heading down. At the edge of the field some of the earth has been dug and made ready for excavating. I drive down a crescent, and all the time I look around but see no-one, not even a wild animal and it reminds me of those ghost towns you see in movies with windows bordered up and fences that need painting. Electrical wires dangle out of place like eels and all but one sign catches my attention and it reads: Barnwell & Sons Realty. Call George Barnwell TODAY!

I remember meeting up with George Barnwell a couple of months back when he came around Smitty's Farm introducing himself and talking a mile a minute about how nice the Brunswick countryside smelled. He had questions about Mr. Smitty, the property, Mum, and this was all in between his storytelling.

"I'm George. The biggest property guy on the planet. I believe I can help you. You now don't have to pay a fortune to get the expertise you need to see your home. I re-engineered almost everything about selling real estate just so I can make your life easier."

I remember conversation between the old boy and George went back and forth like a game of ping pong.

"Well, one thing you can say is there's no denying the value of a good lot of land."

"I would agree, George."

"Especially when its uprooted with gold old Canadian Shield. A by-product from the railroad days back in the late thirties."

"Well before then, George. But I hear what you're saying."

"Sure, I'm going back to Great-Grandpa's neck of the woods."

"That's a long way back."

"Sure it is. But you can't argue that it's still ever present in this very spot we stand."

"This very spot?"

"Sure. I can guarantee it."

"How do you plan to do that, George?"

"Do what?"

"Guarantee it."

"How do you plan to guarantee it?"

"It's my word."

"Your word?"

"That's right."

Needless to say Mr. Smitty refused to let George off the hook and I wasn't in a position to say the least bit.

I enter the Donner Farm gates and drive up.

"So you think she'll leave you something, Alfred?"

"Who?"

"I heard Mum is very sick."

"Oh, she's alright."

"I heard her time is up. Think she might leave you a pretty penny?"

"What do you mean pretty penny?"

"Inheritance. She just might put aside a million bucks for you Alfred." I smile. "Didn't you say she had a real liking for you?"

"Sure."

"People in her position leave money to poor folks all the time."

"None off my back."

"Are you telling me that she's not about to wet your beak a little bit for all that help and care you've given her for the past forty years?"

"Wouldn't be fair?"

"How wouldn't it be fair, Alfred?"

"Just wouldn't."

We entered the slatted wooden gate at the end of the Dawson Road fork with Mr. Smitty's new Ford Ranger recently purchased for sixty thousand bucks. The back of the truck was filled with what Alfred calls "Churks". Once every quarter or so, Alfred and I take a dozen or so Churks around Thanksgiving to the different farms and offer them as a gift or exchange. Churks are spoon fed chickens grown to be as big as turkeys. We try and keep them a secret as best we can but you know how it goes when a good thing goes around. It's not uncommon for me to turn down hundreds of folks who come knocking on Smitty's Farm asking for thirty-pound chickens.

Alfred doesn't see well and needs to squint to see the sign. "What's it say?"

"Closed," I read.

"Well, I'll be damned," Alfred said. "I hope Mum don't find out." He swigs from the thermos that's been resting comfortably in its holder and wipes his mouth with his sleeve. "This is one-before Church Day, ain't it?"

"Yup. Probably away on summer vacation."

Donner Farm is owned and run by the Donner Family. Back in the early 90's, Derek Donner bought old Matt Foley's property and built hen houses. Shortly after, the farm's focus was on lamb breeding and fresh produce farming.

"That bugger never goes on vacation."

Alfred throws me a look: "You think maybe his two weeks is up?"

"I don't know, Alfred. You want to wait around and see?"

We head on out.

A quarter of a mile beyond the Donner Farm gate, Dawson Road ends in a wide clearing. The close-pressing alders and maples give way to reveal a great flat area of raw earth thanks to a fleet of tractors. Beyond this flat area is the gravel pit where current builders are laying their footprints. The rumor' s got a monster developer called Monarch Homes on their way to Brunswick with plans of making the Hornsby Farm into a subdivision of semi-detached homes.

"First come the signs," Alfred says. He rolls up his window and sinks into his seat.

"You think the Hornsby's will sell?"

"Already signed."

Jake Hornsby, owner of Hornsby Farm, was no fool. Not an educated man, he was still aware on some of the key ingredients developers look for when sniffing around for land. He knew how to not get suckered into a bad deal. A well-read man, he knew the advantages of an existing sewer and hydro service to the property, something a lot of the dogs look for in future development. The common rule is provincial and municipal authorities won't allow development in the middle of nowhere. Service and infrastructure are a big part of it. And Hornsby sat but two miles from Truro Hydro with easily accessible routes. Think about how easier it is to get in with those dump trucks and tractors. Think about how much more money a developer can make, and because it ain't getting any easier for these dogs to find land that's not already increased in value they consider it a huge advantage when municipality zoned land is staring them right in the face.

Ten years ago, Tim Huntington who's no more than a stone throw from the Hornsby's thought the fifty acres of land he lived on wasn't good for much. His scrubby plot mainly served as a buffer between his little farming operation and the rapidly-growing suburbs of nearby Truro County. You can't blame Tim for jumping as high as a kite when a housing developer came knocking offering him an astounding $2.8 million for his land. Almost as suddenly as he appeared, the Huntington Farm sign went down. Oh well! Tim wasn't much of a farmer anyway. As the saying goes, take the money and run. I can't say much I'd hate for any developer to buy the Smitty's out.

Then again, who would in their right mind say no to fifteen million bucks?

That was the last offer made by some developer from somewhere down in the States. He planned to chop Smitty's Farm into tiny squares and build custom-made townhomes. Mr. Smitty declined. Or so I heard.

Farmers are a tight lipped bunch of folks. Landowners are even tighter. They don't voice their complaints or desires outside their own circles. Around here, it has always been "tighten the belt and go on" until things improve. But lately, things are not improving. Take the Jackson's Sunflower Farm just up the road, I see more and more folks like Drew Jackson welcoming outside investors. The land is sold at a meager price or the land sits ignored or used as parking lots by out of town truckers. Both of the Jackson boys left Truro for jobs in the city. Drew's on crutches. Farm's dying. Or already dead.

The rest of the country will come to their senses soon enough when corporate holdings become a monopoly and the quality of food is reduced. There's been some talk about Mennonites still making a living on the farm and I think that's great but it's really far and between if you ask me. Although from what Alfred's saying about the Griffith Farm comes from what many Mennonites have been doing across the country which is consolidating and working together and farming larger productive farms to make it pay. Then there's other folks like The Kooks who have taken it to the next level and moved into manufacturing and marketing their own products.

The Kooks Farm is located about twenty minutes from Minden, west of Brunswick County. The Kooks started grading eggs back in the early eighties when there was a demand to local stores. All the eggs that they couldn't sell themselves went to a larger egg station at the end of the week. That gave the Kooks a fresh supply of eggs for our local customers. By the nineties, they had the opportunity to purchase an existing Registered Egg Grading Station in nearby Kirby. This increased their customer base and egg supply. As the story goes they moved from one Grading Station to another each time expanding their capacity by almost four times.

By the year 2000, things started to turn bad for the Kooks. There was just not enough money so in a turn of events they began marketing *Kooked Eggs* which were offered already made and hard-cooked in a variety of recipes. It was a hit from the start and they now currently have *Kooked Eggs* distributed throughout the country in a wide variety of customers that include Cash & Carry Outlets, Restaurants, Bake Shops, Fruit Markets, Fruit and Vegetable Wholesalers, Health Food Stores, Small Grocery Stores, Deli's.

"Now what, Alfred?"

"Too early yet to see Old Homer. Let's go on over to Kurt's new place," he suggests.

"Aren't they up the road?"

I slow down at the approaching traffic light flashing red.

"Turn here by the three headed thing-a-ma-jig!"

Alfred holds up his right index finger and points to the sign that reads: Bishop's Winery.

The main entrance is but a stone throw away.

Alfred and I walk in through the front and I gotta say right off the bat I had no idea that a Smitty could be so smart. I mean, Kurt, Mum's boy, Mr. Smitty's stepbrother, did an astonishing job transforming the old Bishop family barn into a winery. With its big windows and high ceilings and old joists intact it reminded me of an old war museum.

If I haven't already mentioned, this little winery has a counter bar on your right as you walk in - and then on the left is a glassed off area where the wine making happens. They have a few info panels along the wall too, if you're into reading about the process. Alfred and I are lucky we have both Kurt and his wife Stella show us around.

They have a few types of wines here. I try their Merlot in a small cup, and it's really nice - fresh and delicious. We are offered a serving of cheese and crackers on the house to nibble while we drink, which I think makes it.

Other than Merlot, they offer a dozen other types, Cabernet sauvignon (not a fan!), Pinot noir, Barbera (not as popular as the others). There's also some white available – Chardonnay, Sauvignon Blanc, Chenin Blanc.

I wonder about what the word "Sauternes" means, as it's a favourite among sweet wines – it's from Bordeaux. Sauternes comprises almost half of Kurt's sweet wine production, so he points out us. My only gripe is I can't stomach sweet wine. It makes me wanna gag!

Kurt makes a bitter peach flavoured wine that's delicious let me tell'yah. I don't have to worry about paying. We can treat any transaction as an exchange or simply just ask for what we want. When any of the Smitty's are involved it's an unsaid rule that everything is paid for. Saying that, in appreciation we'll throw in a half-dozen churks.

"Hey, Kurt, how did you learn so much about wine?" I ask.

"I read the book," he says.

Kurt can't help talk in heavy sarcasms. He's a victim of the boarding education system. He'd been shipped off to boarding schools all of his life which included a stint at a military academy when he was thirteen. He came back to Arthur's Farm about six years ago to collect on a trust fund left by his old man, Mum's second husband.

I empty another glass. "It's a good book," I say.

"Did you want a case for yourself?"
"Six cases will be fine."
"Red or white?"
"Give me a mix. More Merlot than Chardonnay."
"You know my brother in-law's taste," says Stella.
Kurt adds, "My step-brother likes everything."

Kurt's a great host and Bishop Winery is a great place to visit if you're in the Brunswick area. It's not the Canadian bush but being in the middle of Minden you have to remind folks its past the old Brunswick highway and before Seagram's Gas Stop on 48.

We sample a few more wines.
"How's mum?" Kurt's inquiry is directed to Alfred.
"Mum's holding her own."
"That's not what I heard, Alfred."
"What can you say for a ninety year old?"
"It's hard to watch an old woman suffer."
Alfred is always sympathetic.
"She's holding up."
"Like a building."
"On stilts."
"She'll be fine."
"She'll be dead by Tuesday."
I don't say a word.

We drink some more. As we prepare to leave we're given a couple of extra bottles of wine for ourselves and a couple more to take home as gifts. Stella says they make great gifts for family and friends for all occasions.

Kurt instructs us on what he refers to as "wine maintenance" mentioning that its fine to keep it at room temperature while on our journey home, but it would have a better lifespan getting it back in a refrigerator as soon as possible.

"Will do!"

"Have your family drop by."

"Yes, of course. Thanks again."

On our way out I asked Alfred about Kurt and why he walked with a limp and Alfred said Kurt grew up with a muscle disorder and doctors told him he couldn't run, climb, or jump because his hips were under developed. He said he'd have to get them replaced every fifteen years or so. If he did any of the things he was told not to do the doctors said he'd end up in a wheelchair. It's been this way since he was in 5th grade, and he's forty years old now.

"He's a mean guy cause of it."

"Because of what?"

Alfred lowers his voice. "Cause of them disease. Arthoritis."

"Arthritis."

"Can't blame him being mean. Anybody been mean growing up with arthoritis."

Alfred adds at one time Kurt was forced to wear leg braces.

"You know them," he said, "them steel frames."

"Mum must have been tough on him."

"There was no skipping rope with mum if you know what I mean, let me tell ya."

Alfred speaks with indignation as he goes on: "Kurt worked his tail to get them braces off. Mum didn't care a darn about them braces if they were gonna keep Kurt from applying himself. Just like his sister Josephine who locked herself in her room studying to get them straight A's so she could show her mum her honors class medallion. She liked to show me her report card every June before she showed mum."

"Josephine showed you?"

"Sure she did. I didn't really care for the A's. That was none of my business. But she liked to show me them anyway just so she could work enough muscle before she went to mum."

"How hard was mum?"

"Hard."

"How hard?"

Alfred grimaces with a dizzying chuckle. "Harder than a hard hat."

On our drive over to Gillian's Apple Farm I thought about my own mom. Dad died and then mom began to get sick. It wasn't the first time she got sick, and I thought she was going to get better like every time she got sick but she took a big turn for the worse. By the time I got to her, she was unconscious and I could not talk to her, tell her all the things I wanted to say. Then in a heartbeat she passed on. I began to feel guiltier than ever in my life. There was so much I had to say to her that I never got to say. As time went on, it began to bore a hole in me. I began thinking what I could have done to make things better, was it all my fault? Did I neglect her when she needed me the most? When she had to take care of the funeral arrangements for my dad could I not have been there for her? Dealing with all those bankruptcy lawyers? How could I have abandoned my mom? That's what I was thinking. Then my guilt began to settle in even more. I started having anxiety attacks. I couldn't eat, I couldn't sleep. I began thinking the world would be better without me. Like an unwound clock run on dead batteries. There was no way out. No aid. No involvement. No use. No function. No value. No hope. As the old saying went: "Time had passed me by" and left a sign which read: "No Trespassing".

Unfortunately, every last thread tied to my mother and father remained in the forefront and façade of my mind. They were the times of struggle. They were the times of frivolous spending, hard drinking and unrelenting emotions. My mother and father ran like busy rabbits past their own parent's generation of tired little mice. They saw it as a climb in some regards predating back to the Second World War and the immigration to a new country when millions of mice crossed the Atlantic on an Old Charter run by a government official. It was a flee, an escape, a revolution in some respects that took from the Old World.

In the beginning these mice found the barren of nooks in war homes. They housed two and sometimes three families of mice in one nook, bunked two on a postage stamp and created a philosophy under the pretext of simplicity and survival. The 50s and the 60s were a time when you relied on unions, Elvis Presley and overtime instilling brotherhood, masculinity and a hard work ethic mentality which would finally take to fruition a short decade later when it was time to finally celebrate and reap the rewards of family living.

I grew up in the seventies watching my parents embrace the culture of mid-America with its fascination for Coca-Cola, McDonalds, polyester suits and Disco music. My folks first house was an affordable semi-detached in a neighbourhood at the time was respectively safe from any worries of mass shootings. The homes were built on cinderblock and offered a garden. Families ate supper at the table together every day of the week and TV had taken over the country with daytime soaps and late night TV with Johnny Carson. Looking back at old photos it is a wonderment to see the evolution of the TV in an average North American home from countertop TVs and four-legged models to large consoles and flat-screens.

The home and business computer has become the single most revolutionary invention to date. As did the Ford Model T in the twenties and TV in the fifties, the home computer, especially the Apple Mac, changed society forever by capitalizing on providing what the automobile and TV did prior which was provide insular independence to common folk. As in the early part of the century when horse and cart were the sole source of transportation, when it was quite common to walk to school and work. The automobile allowed the individual to travel alone and see outside the community while TV offered immunity to individual experience. The computer took it one giant leap forward by assisting the individual the access to communicate with the world. Life got bigger. A little bit at a time at first until the eighties came along and those kids born from the Second World War built skyscrapers and suburbs. Many got rich and many lost their parents. That's when my gramps and grams left the planet. The Second World War vets were buried while Apple Inc. took over.

It should be of no surprise that Apple Inc. is the richest company in the world today. Steve Jobs alone made certain of that. No other man in history has influenced society greater in my opinion. Sure you had Columbus, Edison, Tesla and Bell but let's face the facts with Jobs piggy-backing the internet he fortified Globalization with the impact of the IPhone, the single greatest communication device.

6
Metamorphosis Of Greed

Yesterday I heard Teddy planned on coming alone to see me and at first I was disappointed not to see his wife and kids but after some thought I realized it was the wiser approach for now. Teddy said he didn't want to rush into things, he wanted a chance to look around Smitty's Farm and like he used to say when we were kids have an opportunity to investigate. I didn't blame him. With all them snow geese flying overhead it can get pretty foggy out here if you know what I mean. The winters are exceptionally long with the yip of coyotes. The spring and summers can appear even longer after feeling the mosquitoes jab with the razor sharp spear of a cannibal. And the Fall? Well, it can be just that one big downslide of rain and mud and sludge if you don't take the time to pre-plan.

Teddy's expected to arrive around one this afternoon so I've got the whole morning to get my chores out of the way. I'm pretty confident I'll get the opportunity to bring Teddy around to meet everyone and who knows we might just get a chance to do some hunting. Teddy and I had been brought up on waterfowl hunting. The best hunting there was in in behind The Canadian Shield.

Dad would take us up north to a clearing and look for any kind of birds. For us, hunting meant shooting birds. Dad wasn't into prey he called "livestock" which was anything on four legs. He didn't care to blow the guts out of deer or moose or whatever roamed around on the ground. And somehow, I understood what he meant and I'm glad that bird hunting is all that I'm interested in. For a few years there when I was living in the suburbs I stopped hunting altogether. It took Smitty's Farm and a few years to change my thinking but I did and now I look forward to the Fall season as a reaffirmation of nature's bounty and, of course, our position as hunters within nature.

The wind is at 10 mph so it'll be good to look for pheasant. We'll go up to Jake Barclay's Farm. Jake's always been good with short notice and as long as we're wearing the proper gear (hunter's orange) he's good with it.

I'm still relatively new to pheasant, having grown up in a subdivision where the closest we got to shooting season was when the government sent pest-management people to shoot seagulls. Joking aside, there's no chance to hunt in the suburbs unless you want to pick out a fellow suburbanite and his dog walking down the street at hundred yards. There's a story about an old bloat named Joe Hill who liked playing video games by day and sniping stray cats by night. He said he shot the poor critters because he was bored. Another story has a guy, in his early twenties, coming into a Wal-Mart with a shotgun blasting away at random. When the police caught up with him he said he was peeved at the cashier for not giving him the right change. He referred to the cashier as a "pesky wolf trying to short change him". Then there's Jay "Elmer" Fuddle, who decided to climb up to the roof of an elementary school and start shooting at kids saying sometime afterwards that he was hunting "wabbits".

I tried geese recently, loved it, and now am on to the next least scary one on the list of game meats. Pheasant really does remind me of a smaller chicken, but with much leaner meat and a slightly gamey smell to it, which was why I decided to braise it the last time I went out and caught. I used a powerful spicy and tangy Louisiana Hot Sauce mixed with mayo and lemon juice. As with most things I'm unsure about, I went the easy way, low and slow, and the results were deliciously tender. I learned this trick through my mom. We had a regular supply of, mainly ducks, but also other game birds when I was growing up. I remember my mom leaning the cooking pan from side to side when she was making stock or soup with the carcass to check for any lead-shot rolling around inside. Mom had always been a little too cautious and over protective. I remember this one instance a long time ago when she woke me up at five in the morning to look at one of the new neighbour's dogs and she's like "don't trust any dog, Casey". So anyway she went off for the day and she was telling me some things she wanted done around the house and she's like "and don't forget to take a knife in case that mangy dog gets in your way," and I laugh because I think she's joking and then I remembered my mom never jokes and then she's says "no I'm serious if it goes after you, you will have to kill it," and then I'm like well I don't think I could kill a dog. Keep in mind I'm barely five feet tall and just over a hundred pounds and then she looks at me, right in the eyes and says, "if it goes after you, you have to kill it." And I'm thinking to myself, why don't I just walk the opposite way or keep out of his way or don't go far from the house instead of me worrying about taking a knife to his throat. Better yet why don't I just stay in the house for the rest of my childhood?

Anyway, Teddy steps off the Greyhound and looks at me with an expression of confident satisfaction. Don't forget he's my twin so he's picture perfect. For anyone else, they may have said, watching him, holding a small suitcase in his hand and smiling slightly, that here was a man just glad to be away from the rat race of life. He looks also, with his long coat and his cropped hair, as if he'd been at war.

We embrace and he tells me he's starving. In no time we're seated at a local restaurant called Jubba Nubba, one of my favourite places in the world, and look to disembody Brunswick's famous deep dish poutine and Jerk Chicken.

Three tables down stands a short, stout, wheezing waitress, talking and laughing uproariously with a man standing behind her who has one elbow propped on the back of his chair. Now and then Teddy raises his hand for the waitress's attention.

"Excuse me! Over here, please!"

Teddy's somewhat aggressive manner attracts a few ears. He obviously isn't a familiar figure here, and he looks out of place in a white shirt and tie. Like a salesman, he wears his hair short and combed to the side. Had we been sitting in a cafe in New York City, all right; but we're not in New York City. If his aggressiveness isn't enough, he pulls out a wad of bills at the waitress in order to get her attention. And as always he begins every response with "now listen."

Let's just say I do my best to calm the old boy down. I understand. It's been a heck of a long trip; riding fifty-six hours non-stop across the country in a vacuum packed can of sardines. Some things to know for you amateur Greyhound riders, layovers are technically not stops but better described as Rest Points. Somewhere you can get something to eat or do anything else you like except rest. Like stretching your muscles. Taking a good dump. Laying on the grass. Laying on your back is the important thing. Just don't be late! Remember, those bus seats don't recline. Those toilets don't exactly flush. Bring your own pillow and plenty of narcotics – I mean sedatives. Preferably legal ones. And like I said bring a comfortable pillow and you can sleep on the bus or at least try.

"Get any sleep?" I ask.

"Some." Teddy looks around for a very long minute and then reaches into his pocket and pulls out a pill bottle: "I almost forgot."

"What are those?" I say with a smile.

"Anxiety pills."

"You don't need them, do you"?

Teddy is quite aware of how I feel about prescription medicine.

"Sure I do."

The more he shakes the tiny plastic bottle in front of me, the less I want to listen to him speak.

"I have something to tell you," he says.

"What is it?"

At this point in our brief conversation I'm thinking the worst.

"I spoke to God."

Instead of rising from my chair, or closing my eyes, or doing whatever one does when they hear of such nonsense, I keep my head still like a corpse gazing at Teddy and not saying a word... I've heard there's a lapse in time from the moment one sees or speaks to God and before they are taken, there's a time in between, before the body shuts down completely and the spirit takes over. Like death. It begins with the kidneys, then the lungs as they fill with fluid... like the heart that has stopped working like a dead fish out of water it is now the brain's turn.

"I can't quite pin it but I know it was him."

Something is wrestling inside of me. Going back and forth. It has me by the throat. Him? God a him? Why not a her? I sit there perfectly intact, seeing the image of my twin with his children back home. His wife is nowhere to be seen and that realization makes me nervous. They should be together. I should see them both. I have absolute certainty that she'll show – because there is no one else for my brother. That fact I've always known. Not so much by true love. But by nature. Something I believe is much greater than any cupid of love. Just as you are born to die you are born to be with someone or something.

This was true with my mom and dad.

"Is there something wrong with Trudy?"

Trudy is Teddy's wife.

"You don't understand," Teddy insists. "I heard from dad."

"Dad's been dead for ten years."

"Eleven," he clarifies, "Just listen. Would you mind listening to me for a minute without interrupting me?"

"Okay," I say.

I was in bed and I heard these exact commands:

"'Teddy, Teddy – come here.' Wondering at first if it was mom because it sounded like a woman's voice. Not like dads, not a deep voice. The voice came from the doorway. Then came another voice. I asked who it was, and the voice said, 'I'm here to take care of you. I will fix you up. Come with me.' I asked the voice if he was God. The voice responded, 'Quick, come see. You'll find out.' As I proceeded further with questions I received evasive answers. The voice kept giving me a sense of urgency, insisting that I should step through the doorway. With some reluctance I rose from my bed and approached the doorway. Suddenly I was in a thick fog. I can't see a foot in front of me. I repeatedly asked who are you and I hear, 'You'll find out.'

As I walked through the doorway the fog grew thicker and darker, and the voice began to change. At first it seemed rather playful and happy, but when I crossed the doorway threshold, the voice began to get aggressive. 'Hurry up, you're wasting time.' An echo of the voice giggled hysterically as it came closer to me. As I continued to walk, I felt that I was descending. I suddenly thought of Hell and the Devil and began to panic. To my horror I saw a pillar of fire in front of me.

Then I heard the voice again and it told me to pray to Jesus. It started singing things like, 'Lord, you take away the sins of the world.' I was standing there in front of a fire. Then I was told a second time, 'Pray to Jesus' and the voice kept repeating, 'Pray to Jesus'. I don't know why, but all of a sudden I wanted to pray. And I, inside, screamed, 'Jesus, please save me.' That thought was screamed with every ounce of strength and feeling left in me. When I did that, I saw, off in the darkness somewhere, the tiniest little star. The light conveyed to me that it loved me in a way that I can't begin to express. It loved me in a way that I had never known that love could possibly be. He was a concentrated field of energy, radiant in splendor indescribable, except to say goodness and love. This was more loving than one can imagine. I knew that this radiant being was powerful. It was making me feel so good all over. I could feel its light on me – like very gentle hands around me. And I could feel it holding me - And loving me with overwhelming power."

I'm speechless.

"What do you think I should do?"

I say exactly what's on my mind: "Let's go hunting for starters," and for a moment he gazes at me with a cold sullenness like that of a statue. "We can hunt sparrow if you want," I add knowingly that sparrow is my Teddy's favourite.

Teddy remains silent and I immediately break it by saying: "I understand. Can we talk about it later? Your experience sounds fascinating. I want to hear all about it later, okay?"

"Okay," he murmurs.

We chatted the entire way to Jack Barclay's Farm. It's a dense field with plenty of hard marsh to walk. You don't want soft marsh or that weedy stuff found near swamps when you're hunting on foot for more than a day. I prefer it green and hard. When it rains it's even better for walking with the glug and chug you get when the dirt turns to mud. I can't wait for Teddy to step in. It's gonna remind him of Gloucester Park where we used to hunt when we were kids using slingshots to take down pigeons.

We enter an open field and my heart's racing. Teddy's is too. I can tell by the way he holds his shotgun in the upright position, ready to pounce. We cut across what appears to be a narrow ridge so I can angle to where Teddy is pushing the target forward. If everything works right I expect to flush whatever is hiding behind this lofty oak tree about fifty yards in front of us.

Pheasant hunting brings back so many good memories with my dad. Not only did we love to dine pheasant but my dad would enjoy using the browns, and reds and florescent green feathers at his fly tying desk. He was always concocting a new, sure-fire fly to outwit his favourite fresh water salmon.

My dad's favourite shotgun for pheasant hunting was his Remington Model 11. He really loved that shotgun and would even occasionally use it for trap shooting. Loaded with slugs it was a mighty weapon with awesome stopping power.

My instincts are dead on with dad's Remi in my hands and the shot scares a pheasant out of the bush. There's no way of getting a second shot off either so I work around the tree until I can get back into open field. While I trudge on Teddy's barking up at the sky and shooting like Yosemite Sam.

"What the heck are you shooting?" I say.

"Shush!" He replies with mounting irritation. "I can see him; he's almost ready to come out."

I'm too flustered to argue. I'm not the specimen I was fifteen years ago when I could go on for hours and hours and hours. I reach for my bag and pour myself a small cup of coffee from my little thermos. After catching my breath and regaining some internal combustion I push myself to my feet and walk, with

Teddy at heel, back to my Suburban. We haven't been out long but I'm tired. I unload my shotgun, load my bag in the back and then I push myself into the driver's seat and start the truck to let it warm up while I drink more coffee and fish out a candy bar. The total exercise of the walk around the mushy slough, through the cattails and ultimately getting out of the dry grass had lasted exactly one-and-a-half hours. No big deal. The humidity is 14% which means that I've spent much more energy getting a shot off than I'd normally have hitting target.

Our drive back gives us time to catch up and talk about old times in Miller's Creek, mom's fried potatoes and dad's awesome fish deboning. I, for one, miss my parents like crazy. I'd had a chance when we first left to visit their stones but we, my wife and the girls, haven't had much luck in finding the right time to go back. It's mostly my fault and the rest of my family knows it and accepts it. For one thing going back to Beeton Cemetery would mean I'd have to go back to Beeton and I'm not too keen on doing that. Beeton brings back some bad memories for me, even with having a wonderful childhood. I just can't escape that time when I was in my financial hole, you know, that time in my twenties, early thirties when I'd dug myself in real deep.

When Teddy and I return to Smitty's Farm the sky overhead is a brilliant pattern of breezy, washed orange. Like a Van Gogh. I park my Suburban near the main barn. I'm tired. Hunting takes a lot out of you; especially when you miss your target. I look over to Teddy to see if he's shaken up. He's fine. You know I'd promised Teddy I'd make him see how fun it was out here in Brunswick and so far everything's working to plan.

As we make our way up the gravel path I can see Henry, Mr. Smitty's boy, about a seventy-five yards up the road. He's by his lonesome. Then Henry's always by his lonesome. In fact, Henry gives new meaning to the word recluse; sort of how one views seclusion. The truth is Henry Phillip II isn't actually hiding, he's lost. He's searching, and well, so what? He carries on like he's happy as a pig in mud. And that's the important thing, right? So what that he peers up at the sky as though it were about to fall. He's rich and plays a good game of chess.

My wife thinks Henry's off. Then who isn't? Alfred's convinced Henry is too rich for his own good. I don't think too much about Henry other than the fact that he likes hunting geese and cross-breeding exotic birds. Can you imagine cross breeding a duck with a seagull? Blue jays with pheasant? I mean what can anyone expect from a grown man who grew up an only rich child?

"Henry, this is my brother, Teddy."

Henry's head bobs madly in disagreement. "Yeah, sure. That's exactly the sort of thing your brother wants to hear."

I look up at Henry for a moment, smiling gently and then hold out my hand for him to take. "Here you go, Henry. Cut the pinky off and leave me the rest."

"That's just like you, Casey. Hogging all the attention."

He looks past me and stares wildly into the distance. I follow his gaze.

"Where are you from, Teddy?"

"Toronto."

"The big city?"

"Just outside. A place called Beeton. We're about an hour commute."

"I know Beeton," William says. "We had friends in Beeton. This is going way back. I think there were no more than five thousand at the time."

"There's over a hundred thousand now," Teddy adds.

"Beeton was all farm country before the highway."

This is my chance to bud in. "The whole country was one big farm before the highways."

"Highway 10, is it?"

"Yes," Teddy verifies.

I'm glad they're getting along.

"It's expanding everywhere."

"It's greed," I say.

"Sure," Henry counters. It's a counter response. I can hear it in his tone of voice. "But it's necessary."

"Fifty years from now there won't be enough land to grow food."

"Fifty years from now you'll be dead."

"That is true," I say, "but I'm thinking for my children and their children."

"Are you telling me civilization will have to stomach another batch of little Casey's... I don't think we're prepared for that. Let alone the disappearance of farmland. What do you think, Teddy?"

Teddy is lost for words.

"See that, Casey. You've got your own twin tongue tied. I think you should think twice next time you think about hunting up at Jack Barclay's place."

I'm trembling, rooted to the cause so to speak, as Henry's drooling laughter inches up my back.

"Still, farms should not be sold off. They need to be owned and cultivated by those who work them – by people who know their land and who have a stake in improving it."

Henry is still laughing as he walks off, now a good twenty yards away from us. I can hear "communist" under his breath.

In the next hour Teddy and I make our way over to Brunswick Diner for a late lunch. The BLT's are delicious and because I'm a regular the girl behind the counter always gives me an extra strip of bacon. It's a perfect place to sit back and read the funnies which is one of my favourite past times. Plus, the coffee is delicious! I think it's a Costa Rican blend.

While we sit back and enjoy our meal I tell Teddy all about Smitty's Farm and what he can expect to make in dollars. It's important to know he's not just coming out here to run from his problems. Changing his way of life means changing how he sees his life. Whatever I say means nothing if in the end he's not up to making the change for himself and seeing how he can benefit financially and spiritually. I have to know that he made the right decision for himself and his family. Once I let go of the brakes I expect him to go. If he fails to see the upside of this life so be it. That's not what's at stake here. When I freed myself I didn't have any expectations nor did I want any fulfilled. I was sooner happy to just feel freed from my chains and be gone with it.

"What do you think so far?" I say.

"Hunting this morning brought back a lot of good memories."

"I'm glad."

I look over to my brother and I can tell he wants to share something that's on his mind so I sip my coffee and let him go.

"Like the time we were out by Folsom's Creek," he says, "you know, by the old well and these hurricane winds were whipping us from one tree to another. All I could see was your Blue Jays cap walloping in the air and I grabbed at it but I couldn't reach it because it was too high. I jumped and the uproar of the wind through me back again and again. The air smelled of musty cattail dust and the tiny puffs of cattail cotton from the pods being whipped by the melee, were everywhere. You remember?"

I look at Teddy with bulging eyes. "I remember."

"Then we ran into dad and Uncle Tim who were asking us about what was going on and Alex, on his first duck hunt, was watching and hearing something that was loud, mean, and scary as hell. His eyes were open like headlights and he was clutching his H&R Single-shot as if it were all that stood between him and the devil's own cattail demon. I got the leash on Soda and then pushed her out of the way. The raccoon still wasn't retreating and five or ten seconds had passed while I struggled. Holding my shotgun in one hand and trying to aim it, while holding Soda clear, I fired a load of No. 4 steel at about five feet. I thought the load would blow a hole through the raccoon and end the struggle. I missed, or the steel shot was useless, or the raccoon was pumped with so much adrenalin the pellets had no effect. I fired the second barrel and the raccoon dropped."

"You remember all that?" I say.

"Yeah."

"Wasn't it a hoot?"

For the next couple of hours we're brothers again: laughing, drinking coffee, reminiscing about good old times while we venture out and about the barns and stables. Anyone that is interested in raising cattle should plan on having a cow barn like the one I talked the Smitty's into rebuilding just over six years ago.

The truth is cattle don't have to be kept indoors so often, but the barn provides a place to keep cattle comfy if the weather becomes particularly brutal, like it can be with our Canadian winters. It's a place of shelter if one of the herd needs some extra medical attention. The best cattle barns are free stall barns. Free stalls don't have side walls.

"They have plenty of room to stretch and take a leak," I say, "which I can't say for those suburbanites in those cramped subdivisions."

I look at Teddy with staring eyes and he doesn't respond. I add, "I built a manure curb. So they don't have to sit in their own crap."

There are various reasons why a person might want to raise cattle. Some raise large herds to sell, others, like Mr. Smitty, raise cattle for his personal pleasure. He sticks with Hereford and Angus for a couple of reasons. Herefords are great for showing in fairs and Angus tastes good. We usually hang on to a dozen or so females and two strong, healthy bulls. We prefer to go with the AI or artificial insemination route. It's the cheapest and the best option for breeding in my opinion.

The thing that most folks don't realize is the super high cost of feeding these animals. I mean, firstly you want to make certain you have the highest quality hay that you can afford to help keep your cattle healthy, wealthy and wise, right? Well, that takes a heck of a lot.

7

Noah And The Cosmos

I've read many books about money and some are good. A handful of them taught me *How to Save*. Thanks to *The Richest Man in Babylon*. Others told me quite bluntly to *Enjoy Life and Spend Money*. I detested those "Secret" books and those "Get Rich Quick" schemes - the good news being they don't work. The best tip I was ever offered on money was from Mr. Smitty. He said to me one day over a shot of Kentucky bourbon whiskey (I always keep shot glasses in the barn for these inspirational moments):

"Casey, the only advantage to having money is it can help you say no."

At the time I remember Mr. Smitty and I behaving like a couple of schoolboys. It was Friday night and he'd heard about his mum taking a turn for the worse. We sat there on a haystack, in the barn, a keg of Erdinger Kristall and a wonderment of boilermakers in our grasp.

"No, sir?" I said with a mix of confusion and hesitation.

"No to your parents, no to your friends, no to your sweetheart, no to your boss. In fact, I encourage it."

Mr. Smitty went on, "I vacation in the Caribbean twice a year. The people there have nothing compared to what we are blessed with here in Canada. They are the most joyful, optimistic, friendly, loving, grateful people I have ever met. Their faith in God is absolutely unwavering. I always leave there feeling so humbled that I would even consider feeling sorry for myself or complaining over stupid little things. I come home being totally humbled and thankful for the things we take for granted like running water, electricity, air conditioning, food, shoes, a spacious home. These people have what we don't have. Deep relationships, hope, joy, love, faith, peace. Sometimes I think they are richer than we are as we have a tendency to put more importance on stuff than substance."

I was touched by Mr. Smitty's words and quite honestly surprised by them. He didn't strike me as a man who spoke so deeply. Of course, I knew he loved to tell stories. He shared them with us any chance he got. One of his favourites was a story all about his trips into the English countryside. The green and brown fields, gentle hills, hedgerows, clean blue skies... A huge pheasant sitting in the powdered field... Bright golden daffodils at the roadside... Clouds of white blossom in the orchards... The works of Jane Austen... The story of a newlywed couple found dead in a well in Leicestershire on their honeymoon.

I remember the night he told the Leicestershire story. It was a warm night, a cigar smoking night, a moony night. Mr. Smitty had his banking colleagues over and me, Dora, Liza, Beatrice and some of the other hands helped out. I caught the introduction of the story on my way into the study topping up the gentlemen's snifters. Mr. Smitty quit drinking hard liquor years ago but he enjoyed the odd glass of vermouth when his friends were over the house.

"Folly Town was filled with reliable folk who could always be counted on. In the case of Benjamin Hillier, regarded by those who knew him intimately, reliability was not something that came easily for "Benjie". Those who knew Benjie's parents, particularly Mum, knew Benjie's antagonist view of life resulted from dear old Mum's antagonist approach to rearing her only boy, in her own words saying about her son, 'You could never get Benjie to wipe his own runny, filthy nose. It was torture with all those germs lurking about.' When asked about Mum, Benjie had this to say, 'Mum? Mum is a bitch. A cold-hearted narcissist who when I had a miserable cold used to wipe my nose using her day old, blood-stained pussy rag just to get even with me.'

Storytelling is a characteristic of being the man Mr. Smitty wanted to be: a creative man; a noble man; a man of courage and fortitude; a man who cared to the welfare of others; a not so ideal man.

Three years after I arrived in Brunswick when the girls were old enough to walk, Mr. Smitty took my entire family to the Scottish Highlands. We saw the highest mountain in the British Isles called Ben Nevis. We went to Inverness and as far as Nairnshire, to Ross-shire on foot up a trail to a medieval castle, Carbisdale Castle, overlooking the river Kyle, where we drank Highland Single Malts and listened to old ghost tales, myths and legends. Carbisdale Castle houses priceless paintings and a collection of beautiful marble statues. One of these statues has an intriguing mechanism whereby on rotating it a hidden door below the Great Staircase opens to a secret passage in the Lower Gallery – it's quite spectacular.

We sailed to the Isle of Mann, bathed in hot springs, and snorkeled in icy lakes, where we saw trout swim beneath us.

I felt drawn into the Highland stories after that. And for years I felt indebted to Mr. Smitty for his great hospitality and care he showed to me and my family. I wanted to reach up and kiss Mr. Smitty and say, "Thank you, thank you!"

But it wasn't the least bit necessary. Mr. Smitty wasn't interested at all. He is a man of no praise. Unlike the rest of us, he is secure. Most men are faced with major failure to meet their goals and need the boost of praise to get by. The male ego denies any weakness and yet it constantly needs to be supported by praise. Men like Mr. Smitty are used to setbacks and take them in stride, very much like a marathon runner. They have the satisfaction of accomplishing little goals and take the strains of pain and negativity better. Although they compete to some degree they usually are not in the grind like other men.

So what am I saying here, that Mr. Smitty is certainly not "superfluous", perhaps "super-extraordinary"? I'm not sure to be honest. I can only speculate about his character as I'm not him. But I can say one thing and even though I'm only hypothesizing I'm pretty sure it has something to do with the environment in which he was raised. I'm aware of some details on his grandpa but I don't know the specifics like how he felt about his father dying in battle or what he ate for breakfast growing up?

Did Mum tuck him in? Were his schoolteachers pleasant to be around? Did he enjoy holidays? Did he celebrate his birthday? Was Old Smitty frugal? Was there music or poetry in the house? At what age did he lose his virginity? There are countless questions that determine an environment.

That being said, there are some common characteristics among the rich, however we want to slice and dice the facts. For example: most rich kids are made aware very early on of something called "old money" or "money inherited".

Tons of them come from the Upper East Side of Manhattan; Boston's Back Bay and Beacon Hill; London's North Shore suburbs or along the banks of Nice and Monte Carlo. The truth is old money is everywhere: in Canada, New Zealand, Germany, South Africa, China, Pakistan, Costa Rica, the good old USA. The ironic thing is "old money" is almost always descendants of "new money" which was originally coined to describe: nineteen century industrialists or bankers like Old Smitty.

A great example lies in a few of the wealthiest families today, i.e., The Rockefeller's and The DuPont's:

While founder John D. Rockefeller had modest origins and was initially considered "new money", he made billions of dollars in oil in the late 19th and early 20th centuries. Over time, the Rockefeller's became considered "old money" as their wealth was passed down from generation to generation and their lineage still remains wealthy.

The DuPont family fortune began in 1803, but they became an extraordinarily wealthy family by selling gunpowder during the American Civil War. By World

War I, the DuPont's produced virtually all American gunpowder.

So what's that saying about the Rockefeller's and the DuPont's? Well, I don't know any Rockefeller or DuPont's but the one thing I can tell you about the Smitty's like so many "old money" constituents is they simply don't view education as the be-all-end-all, mostly because their wealth and connections can already open doors themselves and for their kids that the poor have to struggle to pry open. Mr. Smitty attended private school for years and graduated with a degree in economics only later taking up a position of authority in one of his father's insurance companies. William, Mr. Smitty's uncle, attended all the big schools only to accept an executive position in one of his dad's companies. Hugh, one of Mr. Smitty's first cousins (you haven't met him) scored an IQ score of 200 and planned to attend Harvard on a mathematics scholarship. He planned to work at NASA. But a drunken night in university and two charges of assault had him flee Dodge to some quiet French village until the heat was off. He lived quietly after that and took a position running one of the family's vineyards.

Rich kids, we hear, have it all. Money. Connections. Top educations. Cars and clothes. For those who are part of what Warren Buffett calls "the Lucky Sperm Club," life is supposedly one long shopping trip with a no-limits ATM card.

But what happens when the money runs out?

This notion that old money dissipates can be argued. Someone like William has no plans to marry or have children. So we can assume one day when he's dead and buried and gone from this world his money will also perish. Or once an old money family fortune starts to move down to the next generation, some of it goes with the females, like Mr. Smitty's step-sister, Josephine, who married and divorced into other family lines. When you get enough generations going forward where old money applies, it's safe to say that neither a specific surname applies. Where now you have the Rockefeller's, DuPont's and Smitty's you may soon find them being Rossi's, Klum's and Wong's.

There's the story of the Abram's who were prominent and rich and owned tons of cattle farms in Brunswick. I met one of the sons who was a direct descendant named Eric Hyndman. He dressed well and drove a nice enough car and when I asked him if his Ferrari was parked in the garage he laughed and told me he sold the Ferrari for a Ford Esquire. The money was pretty much gone within the family. It was stolen, squandered and snorted. The family had a much unpublicized legacy of divorces, lawsuits, suicides and murders. His grandmother on his father side was married an unheralded eleven times.

He went on to say that his immediate family which included him and his younger sister were virtually poor on paper. Mainly because his parents spent their lifetimes determined to have everyone think they were vastly better off than they really were. It was a facade.

Today, Eric has never returned to his home in Newfoundland since leaving for boarding school in Vermont many years ago (boarding being another insane family indulgence). Today he is an anonymous lower middle manager in a huge Quebec company, living in a cozy two-bedroom condo that has no view to speak of but which he adores anyway.

I personally believe part of the reasons the Smitty's are still going strong is that there's a built in safeguard to the family trust. If you are a DuPont and you gain from the family trust, your children won't similarly, if your parents collected, you won't. The wealth skips a generation, giving it time to regenerate as it were.

I knew a woman belonging to the Pendleton family (cattle feed fortune) who admitted to me one night over a pint of ale that she never loved her husband (hog slaughtering fortune) when she married him back in the 1940's, but it was such a good match and both families were so in favor of it, that she went along with it. The combined fortune was 100 million plus, and the point of her story was that she had grown quite fond of him, even learned to love him, over the years. (Yes, she was pretty drunk when she spilled it to me.)

The theory of inherited wealth is that you live on the interest from your investments, don't ever dip into the principle or sell off your assets if at all possible, marry strategically to bring more money into the family without lowering its social status, and educate your children carefully so that they follow the same path as you. Since this goes against pretty much every idea that contemporary North Americans live by, you can see why we don't have many old money families. A friend of mine who is a lifelong Quebecer says that the old money rich there are more or less invisible. They don't flash their money around or so things that would get themselves mentioned in the media.

You won't find either Mr. or Mrs. Smitty at your local grocery store shopping for milk and eggs. Not because they're snobbish or overbearing. They prefer that their hired hands run the grocery errands. Sure, you might find Mr. Smitty lodged behind a book aisle at one of the local Starbucks in town but very rarely. Mr. Smitty likes to keep himself out of the hustle and bustle of everyday life and traffic. Although you will find him usually in a private box at the local college watching a junior league hockey game or downing a pint with his Alumni buddies over at King Henry's Tavern. Mrs. Smitty loves to shop. You just won't find her at the mall. When she's looking for a new pair of boots there's a good chance its coming straight from 5th Avenue.

I'm starting to think the main difference between the Smitty's and the rest of rich folks is this flashiness you find. No need for mansions and sports cars when you're filthy rich. There's nothing to prove.

Money is a powerful weapon. It has advantages and disadvantages depending on how you perceive to use it. One advantage of money is survival. With money, you can support yourself. Money provides purchasing power. It is used to buy food, pay the rent or mortgage, pay for medical attention and send the children to college or university. If you do not use the money wisely, there will be disadvantages. Greed of money, or the lack of it, can cause someone to fall off the edge of a mountain, if you catch my drift.

Mr. Smitty innately understands the poor. He knows how much the poor want money. He's seen how money has made the poor very angry. He understands what it is to be poor. He knows of the daily rituals and the beliefs of the poor. Being poor is hoping. Being poor is going without; relying on people who don't give a damn about you. Being poor is s bathtub you have to empty into the toilet and needing that thirty-five percent raise. Knowing you're being judged. Having to say you're sorry more often. Having memorized the Lord's Prayer. Being poor is a cough that doesn't go away. Mixing up frozen canapés with Caviar.

The Smitty's are well aware of all these things and thousands more. He is well aware because he knows them. He's around them. He's welcomed them into his home and given these folks a living and for that reason alone he knows more about poor folk than most rich folk, or any folk for that matter.

"Casey, I was wondering if you would do me a favour?"

"You want me to run over to Salinger's and fetch you a corn beef sandwich."

"Nothing like that."

"It's about Josephine."

"Your sister?"

"Lovely girl. Smart too. Sometimes too smart for her own good." He poured me another shot. "My sister has always been a little on the sneaky side. You know we have photographic evidence of her digging throughout the trash when she was only six years old, hair sticking up every which way, eyes wide, mouth hanging open. I used to say that girl is bright, that girl has an enormous future ahead of her but I'll tell you she can be so sneaky. And hypocritical as well, for instance, today, she came into my study without asking and started annoying me. Whenever I go in her private space without asking she goes off on a tangent and I can't quite understand it. The point is I just can't trust her sneakiness and in under normal circumstances I wouldn't be bothered by it so much but with mum being so ill it's beginning to put a damper on things if you know what I mean."

"I understand," I said. Then he continued:

"I know she behaves like most sisters, and I'm probably at fault because she idolized me and craved my attention for so many years. This is what children do they crave attention from everyone and anyone and are jealous of anyone in the way of what they want, children are quite selfish because they are not yet ready to put others first. We were all young and immature once. It was my sister who got me in trouble. I'm the eldest and their twins so they always stuck together.

"Kurt and Josephine?"

"Yes."

"I didn't know they were twins."

"I bet you didn't know they're my half twins. They're father died a ways back and came along with my mum's second marriage. Anyhow, once those two, Josephine and Kurt, drunk half a bottle of wine and blamed me, because I was barely fifteen at the time my mum thought it was me even though I swore I had not touched it. Another time they got all the food out of the cupboards and put it all in the garden to play shops but there was cereal all over the grass and loads of other stuff, I got blamed for that too. Without going into too much detail I'll just say my sister has always been self-absorbed. She constantly talks about herself and always makes every conversation about her thoughts on things. Well, I have my own thoughts on things too. Additionally, she lies and changes stories to make herself sound better. The point is some time back she met a colleague of mine, Jeffrey's, twin brother, Clifford, out at a bar. Jeffrey's a successful lawyer. They ended up getting really drunk and going home together. Clifford and Josephine. This happened a couple of times and next thing you know they are dating. Not that it was any of my business but it's become very annoying with her dating Clifford as she's become very nosey about mum's will and it's made my wife and I very nervous. This would not be an issue, but I'd given very specific instructions that she see to that mum not be disturbed. It seems quite ridiculous in fact. I don't know why she acts as though she's entitled. I don't really want to make a big deal out of it but I have to behave responsibly and my relationship with my family must remain intact from the good and evils. Do you understand?"

"I understand," I said.

"I'm a little worried about Josephine and this Clifford fellow. I want you to keep an eye on both of them. Tell me where they go and what they do. Just point form notes. I don't need a novel. And keep your distance. At least until mum is gone."

"Sure thing."

8
Time Is A Naked Design

I was rewarded with a new Ford S50 for my duties. In all I'd spent the better part of four days keeping a close eye on Josephine and learning no more than she likes to leave the house early, drop back to the farm for lunch with her kids, dart out for the mid-afternoon and arrive back for a late supper.

I didn't see Clifford the entire time and besides the nanny there weren't any unfamiliar faces. I wasn't too surprised. I'd known Josephine for years and she was what you categorized as "rich common". She often met with friends for breakfast, played tennis at an exclusive club, drove a Bentley and Jaguar, shopped in expensive boutiques, flew to cities like Paris and Milan on a whim, drank champagne for lunch and attended the theater at night.

I've been trying to figure out how I can get Teddy involved without tipping the pot so to speak. Those cop shows always say that when you're getting hot on a trail, you should not invite company. I think that's a good idea, but it doesn't solve my problem. Even with an upset tummy and a bit of a head cold I'm committed to do what I need to do for Mr. Smitty.'

I start my car and drive off.

My foot is riding the pedal softly almost like a leaf fluttering in the wind. I edge onto the gravel pathway and notice the front door to Josephine's house open. I brake. I'm okay behind a big elm. I'm far enough away, at least the length of a football field. Josephine and her kids walk out. I got to be honest, I'm in knots. Yesterday she ran errands in town with her boy Samuel. The day before, she'd spent the entire afternoon with her daughter, Violet, at Chuck n Cheese. Earlier in the week, she stepped out with her friends. If there's one thing that can be said about this woman is she loves to go out.

Josephine's nanny is everywhere she is when she's out with the kids. I don't know her name. I think she's Vietnamese or from Thailand. Is that Thailandeese? It doesn't look like the nanny does a very good job either. The kids always look like they just ran through a car wash. Violet's hair looks tangled and Samuel's shirt is never tucked in. Little Samuel is getting big, though. So she must be feeding him. The last time I saw him was eight months ago, I think, when he was barely out of his diapers. He's a cute kid. But I think they spoil him. He seems to always have a sucker in his mouth. I don't know. Maybe I'm just old-fashioned?

Yesterday I overheard her and her nanny conversing in the kitchen. Well, it wasn't so much conversing because all I heard was Josephine's questioning and the young girl's stuttering appraisals. I saw the burners going and the entire family huddled about the dining room table so I suspected it was suppertime.

"Can you get me that? My arms hurt."

"Sure I can."

"Is the soup ready yet?"

"I'm sure it is."

Ring.

"Can you get that?"

"Sure I can."

"Hello."

I can't make out anything more. During her time on the phone she has her back to me. Click.

I suspect its good news. Josephine yanks her son up from his chair and knocks over a tall glass of milk. She then starts cheering and clapping. The nanny must've thought her boss won the jackpot.

"Can you clean that?"

She's also a complete slob, leaving a disaster in her wake---there's nothing she touches that is in its place after her. There should be a call out for Hurricane Josephine! There's a trail of used tissues, clothes, dishes, blower cards from magazines and other things left behind her. She never leaves anything as neat as she found it. When she gets mail she just opens it all up and leaves it on the table for the housekeeper. She always has stuff everywhere in the bathroom and the counter. Sometimes she doesn't even flush the toilet after number 2's. She claims to forget. I'll sneak in the house from one day to the next and the living room that the housekeeper just cleaned will be a mess. She lets her son pull stuff out of everything like all the DVD's and Video games and lets the nanny take care of it. She just sits there and zones out on TV half the time. She will never shut the doors all the way to the rooms so you find you are having to constantly shut doors behind her (bathroom, laundry room). Just yesterday she cleaned up the den by throwing everything out in the garage in a gigantic hamper she bought so she wouldn't have to do laundry or put it away. Then she wants the housekeeper to be so proud of her for finally picking up her clothes, even though everybody knows it will be a disaster in a few hours again... All this is just a few examples. I don't even want to get into the new Jag she bought five months ago that's always cluttered inside and she has never washed it.

My daughters have full access to all the luxuries on the farm but they have chores they are responsible for. Becky unloads the dishwasher and cleans the bathrooms while Charlotte puts away the dishes and folds the laundry. It's that kind of trade off. Every now and then I mow the lawn for my wife. Becky will vacuum when Charlotte's babysitting. `Charlotte`s thirteen and Becky's sixteen so Charlotte has to respect the fact that Becky is at that age where boys mean something different.

Okay, I take back what I said about having Josephine shackled and shot. It's just that I don't understand this woman. I mean I understand she has no concept of self-sacrifice or that she feels in anyway indebted to her own dignity. Besides all that, she really has me puzzled. I mean I think she's bipolar. Like my mom.

My mom was thirty two years old when she was diagnosed and from what I have learned the younger you are at onset of symptoms the worse your case is. My mother had gone through times when she thought medicine (Haldol) was sugar pulls and she stopped taking them. There are shadow people outside the house and she can hear them talking about her and telling her she is evil. The people on the TV are talking about her and saying the police are coming to get her and take her to jail. She actually had real surgery on her neck to have a chip in her neck removed so she couldn't be tracked.

I always thought my mother used her disease as a cover to her real problem, which was her distrust towards her family. Since the time I was a young child, I have had a tumultuous relationship with my mother. Throughout the years, I have realized that my mother is seen a certain way by family, and a different way by work friends and the general public. She put up a front, often "Martha Stewartesque," where she is the ideal hostess, best worker, ideal mother, dearest friend. But living with her is another beast. She was a regiolect you might say, and spent a large part of her time complaining, yelling, swearing, at anything and everything. She went on rampages about her work situation, supervisor and coworkers. For years she watched political TV shows and ranted at the television constantly.

When I was a child, if she came home from work, and the dishes had not been done, or no one fed the dog, she would scream and complain how she was the only one who did anything around the house. We were always expected to get good grades, and if we got anything below a B+, she screamed at us, and likely grounded us. I was always given punishments that were over the top for the crime. Being grounded for months was written on the large kitchen calendar on the fridge black marker in all caps for everyone to see.

It was humiliating.

9

The Diel Apparatus

A pub can be a great place to relax if you know how to go about doing so. Depending on the people and the environment, getting and keeping a person's attention can be quite a challenge.

It doesn't matter that the pub is Scottish or Irish, or that it carries imported beer, or named after a famous writer. It's not even that important that it's hidden away in a basement or cave. But that it is not difficult to converse with someone in case there are sardines around you. By that I mean if the place is cramped. See, I hate crowded spaces. Unlike my Teddy who is not the least claustrophobic.

When I first arrived in Brunswick I'd heard about a local pub called The Bump and Grind, a pub situated on one of the less busier intersections in town. I took a drive. From the outside, it seemed like your ordinary, everyday run of the pub. That fellow Eric Abram I spoke of earlier; I met him at The Bump and Grind. He wasn't drunk or anything, but he had a few, and talked like a TV analyst while the hockey game was on.

"Do you like hockey?"

"Sure," I said.

"I don't."

I smiled at Eric. "What do you watch it?"

"Who's watching the game? I'm only interested in the commercials."

I started laughing half way through the analysis and he looked me straight in the eyes. I would have turned away normally but he had this terrible cough and I offered him a throat lozenge and he took it. We talked into the night after that and now we're good friends.

Here is some pub history. Let's call it Pub 101. Okay, the Brits have been drinking beer since the invention of the bronze-tipped arrowhead, but it was with the arrival of the mighty Romans that the first inns were built. First came Inns to eat and sleep, then came pubs, as a place to smoke, play darts and get drunk. I won't get into how pubs turned into saloons and taverns with all the raucous or how it spiralled out of control with nightclubs and discotheques.

Teddy and I sit at the Bump and Grind bar and smoke. I'm feeling better being in the company of my brother. The last few days have been exhausting and I suspect the next few more will be even more. I take out my wallet and start looking for Clifford's address that Mr. Smitty gave me. Finally I find it. His house is in town, but I don't feel like driving alone tonight so I'll ask Teddy to ride with me. Mr. Smitty said Clifford used to be in law enforcement so it's important I don't get in too close to his house. He said there might be dogs. Anyway, I order a couple of shots using Mr. Smitty's credit card.

"Two boilermakers, Bartender!"

I raised my arm with a big smile.

"Have you met my twin brother?"

The bartender's name is Ted. He looks a lot like Tom Selleck; just not so tall.

"Pleased to meet you, Teddy."

Teddy barely replies, almost mumbling: "Likewise."

I'm worried. Teddy isn't his usual perky self. In fact, the other day, Shirley said something about Teddy locking the door to Charlotte's room and sleeping in until the early afternoon.

"Hey!" I say. I raise my voice so that he'll hear me the first time.

Teddy nods.

"What's the matter?"

"What?" he says in a low voice.

That response annoys me a little bit. "What do you mean what?" I say. "You're on vacation. You should be happier than a bear in the woods."

"I'm fine." he says dryly.

"You don't sound fine. How about you and I take a ride into town? I have to run a little errand for the old boy and we can sit and chat."

"Where are we going?"

"In town. Not far from here," I say. "Take us but twenty minutes or so. I'll show you the Northern Lights if they're out. You'll love it."

"I don't think the Northern Lights are out this way."

You can tell Teddy's in a bad mood.

"Are you sore at me for being out so much?"

"No," he says.

"Normally it wouldn't be this way," I say. "It's just Smitty has me doing something top secret."

Teddy grins.

"It's not really top secret. I'm just not obliged to say."

"Obliged?"

"Yeah, you know. Rich folk stuff," I say.

"Does it have anything to do with the old lady dying?" he says. "What's her name?"

"Mr. Smitty's Mum."

"Right."

I'm confused. "What do you meaning dying," I clarify. "Dying as in dying or dying as in dead?" I'm trying to be as clear and as calm as I can.

"She's dead."

"Dead?"

"She died this afternoon while you were out."

"She can't be dead."

"She's dead alright."

"How did you hear?"

"Shirley told me over dinner."

"How come nobody told me," I say.

"You couldn't be reached."

"I don't have a cell phone," I say quietly. Then there is a long pause. "I guess that's why Josephine was so happy. She must have gotten the news when she answered the telephone."

"Who?"

For a long minute I didn't know how to answer my brother. I wanted to tell him where I'd been and what I'd seen but I had to figure it out first for myself.

Teddy and I drive to Clifford's and park the rental across the street.

The thing that stinks about being a private eye is having to sit in your vehicle for a long stretch of hours. I understand the importance but its fantastically boring and I can't stand to see another donut.

Teddy didn't seem to mind sitting in the dark. It must have reminded him of our days in my parent's cellar where we used to play a game called "Solitude". The basic idea of the game was that you had find a place to hide and keep quiet for a whole hour. And if you left the place before the hour was up, you had to give up a dollar or candy or something we valued.

I was better at it. I didn't mind sitting in the dark, and I guess that's one of the reasons I'm not scared to be alone in a strange place.

"Did you think mom was a schizo?"

"Who?"

"Mom," I say.

"Where did that come from?"

"Oh, you know how we used to talk about mom's problems, how terrible her temper was, how she didn't trust dad, how she use to lock us in the bathroom when she wanted to punish us, the time she stayed out all night because she said she thought she saw a ghost, all that sort of stuff."

"What about it?"

"Did you think she was schizophrenic?"

He pauses to think.

"I think she was definitely abusive," he continues hesitantly, "I don't think she was schizophrenic."

"What about the delusions?"

"I think they were more narcissist than schizophrenic."

"How come dad never stood up to her?" I ask.

"I think dad didn't want to alienate the whole family," says Teddy.

"Do you think about mom?"

"Yes."

"Do you remember how she used to hiss like a cat when she was mad?"

"How can I forget?"

"She's had quite a lasting effect on us, hasn't she?"

"So has dad."

I nod.

"I think we inherited quite a bit from them both."

I planned to ask "Like what?" but I don't bother. Instead I reach for my beer.

10
The Worm Diary

We all come across that threshold in life when someone close to us passes on. There are so many spiritual and practical matters that need attending to, even in the midst of one's grief.

Mum died at approximately 6:44 p.m. Nearly forty-four hours after I'd spoken with Mr. Smitty. She passed away peacefully with her family by her bedside, and while I missed performing the initial duties of calling the coroner I made up for it in the post-mortem preparations.

Mrs. Smitty took care of notifying family and friends personally. It helps to have several people making calls, to spare one person the full burden, but Mrs. Smitty wanted no part of sharing the burden. We didn't have to worry about organ donating or any last wishes Mum left. I contacted a funeral home in town owned by one of Smitty's close friends and made burial arrangements. The rest was none of my concern. These were matters regarding the deceased's finances and assets – wills, estates, probate, taxes, insurance, trust funds, Social Security, bills, credit cards, retirement accounts, and so on.

Rumour had that Mum was very clear in her will. That her money be distributed using trust funds primarily. In order to help reduce estate taxes and establish supervision over all parties involved.

Mr. Smitty and his step-siblings would stand to inherit well over fifteen million apiece. William and his sister, Sarah Ann, received ten million. Josephine's kids in excess of five million in trust. The rest of us got zero, notta, nil.

This is testament to the wise old aphorism that simply states: "The rich get richer and the poor get poorer" due to Percy Bysshe Shelley. Stories you've read and films you've seen depicting poor hapless fools inheriting a pile of cash simply isn't true. When we speak of ritual we can expect nothing less than natural rationalization in effect. There is loyalty in wealth no matter what we think, as there is with poor folks. People are still people. Rich or poor.

The distribution of the Smitty estate was clearly written from Mum who had a fondness for journal "wittling" (she called writing "wittling") and clearly specified with the following:

"Being in sound mind I bequeath all my money and assets to no less than anyone in my bloodline. Non-blood related need not inquire. Thank you very much."

Mum was buried in nearby Troy at the Mormon Pioneer Memorial Monument Cemetery. It's a private cemetery reserved for mostly wealthy Christians. Old Smitty is there. Old Smitty's dad is there.

Most of the Smitty family attended the funeral. Mr. Smitty's Uncle Preston was there. So was Uncle Phillip and Auntie Mable. Friends and old hands attended. The Caber boys were there.

The Caber's worked for the Smitty's for years. Old Man Caber used to do what I do today. He and his wife lived in our farmhouse and raised two boys, Malcolm and Ernest. Old Man Caber's wife came from a well-off family: her grandmother sitting on five million worth of farmland, but because of the family drama when grandma died they pretty much got nothing. Uncles and cousins fought for years over the farmland, mismanaging and damaging personal finances, creating abusive relationships. When Old Man Caber turned sixty he was diagnosed with liver disease and given six months. One night he and his wife went out cruising in the freezing rain and smashed into a Ford F-150 Platinum killing them both instantly. The story goes that Old Man Caber crashed the car on purpose in order to collect on that $1 million dollar life insurance policy. "It was worth dying," he would have said, "so my boys could inherit a better life." We're not sure to this day if the missus was in on the insurance policy idea.

You can't blame folks too much for being down and out. When you're down and spending lots of money on fancy toys or making a fantasy out of a dream, being stubborn and absent-minded is a very handy defence mechanism. It lets you forget the way life really is. Blind folks like Caber hold onto a dream until it's too late. They truly believe in the dream. What they don't realize is the dream is a figment of their imagination. Too bad Old Caber was too quick in pulling the trigger. Someone should have advised him that there are always choices in life. With that being said it came as no surprise when I heard the Caber boys blew most of the million on women and cars. I said Hi to both Malcolm and Ernest and we briefly exchanged a few words. Some laughs but mostly quiet "oohs" and "wows" considering the circumstances.

When I first told my brother about Mum's death and the second hand stories about the inheritance and the jealousy surrounding it he didn't seem all that surprised. Yet something puzzled him, and he asked me how I felt about the Smitty's keeping the hired hands out of the will. I told him that people were free to choose, and besides Mum's death was a private matter. "We are outsiders in the grand hierarchy," I said.

I remembered when I first arrived to Smitty's Farm and Jim Thompson, Mr. Smitty's nephew, had taught me a thing or two about family hierarchy and how a big guy in a dirty old raincoat can often win when sharing the same surname as the owner. He'd turn up for work carrying a bottle in a brown paper bag, but saying nothing about it---it was just there on the dashboard with no apology or comment---not at all interested in putting me at ease except to offer me the bag, which I declined, making no gestures whatever, except maybe that I was annoyed.

One afternoon we drove out to Truro and he'd taken the liberty of telling me his life story. I recall vividly but I remember how he told it. Like he was on the verge of crying. He'd taken five years and a hundred and twenty thousand dollars to decide that university wasn't in the plans. There were two reasons why he returned home, part of which was some talk about meeting a girl and the other over his trust fund. He kept fidgeting. While we talked he continued referring to Mum as the Old Hag.

"I was promised thirty five thousand by that Old Hag but that never happened."

I told him I didn't appreciate Mum being called an Old Hag and he stopped.

One other time, a Sunday, we took a few of my rifles over to a local gun club and fired at their range. It surprised him that someone who'd spent so much time in the city could be such a good shot.

"Gee, Casey, you belong in a war."

He liked the way I shot; with my high arch and straight elbow. Called me Sniper. He was very complimentary about my technical ability. But he wanted me to shoot further. "Try 750 yards, Casey, using a scope. You won't ever look back." An odd request from a marksman, who was, in my opinion, naturally gifted, and believed that scopes were only for amateurs. He'd noticed my Remington again the night before he left, and was reluctantly suggesting for the tenth time that it was time to bury the old boy.

"You outta come out west with me. Plenty of paying jobs out there. Make twice the amount."

"I can't desert Mr. Smitty," I said.

"Boy, Casey, you're so loyal. Anyway, what were we talking about?"

"Guns."

It drove him nuts that I didn't go automatic. There were five semi-autos alone in his collection, all loaded, and he'd move from station to station firing rounds and hitting at will.

"Casey, listen to me: It's only a very limited situation here. There's nothing for you in the long run. I mean, you're not in the will."

"I know, Jim, but..."

"Casey, I'm telling you, it's a mistake for you to stay. You don't know the Old Hag like I do. We're better off when she goes. Believe me."

This was the young man who lived by the following epitaph: *Keep your friends close, your rich friends closer.*

He gave me a gun demonstration using the rifle in the way Lucas McCain did. When he was finished with the routine, he gave me a big hug and disappeared into the night.

I sometimes thought that he lived by his aversions, Jimmy Boy, and worse off, by haste and even carelessness to details. His mouth was especially revolting. Hypocrisy was not some petty human foible, it was the corrupted essence of fear and greed, which for Jim was purely manifested. Let's face it Jimmy Boy was a spoiled brat---with a heck of a shot!

With that being said, I liked him. And I was saddened when he left for Austin, Texas and not too long afterward died in a domestic shooting incident.

11
Life On An Ant Farm

Teddy left some days after Mum's burial. His send-off was erratic and disjointed - so much that I was forced to apologize. In saying that I was glad we'd gotten a chance to hunt.

I love duck hunting. The entire ritual from starting with a big early 4:30 a.m. breakfast joined by friends and family to gearing up, rigging decoys, pouring that cup of coffee while waiting for legal shooting time to arrive is special to me.

I'll normally spend the entire night before prepping my 12-gauge. The professional's definition of the ultimate duck gun is a 12-gauge semi-automatic for the following reasons: a 12-gauge action allows me to quickly get off a second and third shot and a little extra firepower. On the flip side, my Teddy swears by pump shotguns. He finds them reliable and easy to clean. When it comes to firepower it's enough to blow the head of a resting mallard clear off.

Teddy is the best duck caller. He's a natural. I can't say the same about myself. Ducks have a pretty good ear, and a few sour notes may mean the difference between a hit and a miss.

There were so many birds the day Teddy and I headed out. We headed for the large sloughs north of town. In the light of the sun I could see the pointed forms that were mallards, dozens of them, in their typical V-formation. We lay on our backs and realized we were suddenly in range.

"Do you see them?" I said, and pulled up my Remi.

"Over to the left, I see them."

Hunting, we often like to claim, is about bringing it to bag—killing the specimen. It is within that act, the kill, that each of us, as the hunter, must demonstrate our nobility as a modern predator and dignify that animal's death by our satisfaction of accomplishment.

"Take the shot," I encouraged Teddy. He smiled and pulled the trigger.

Later on the drive home I asked Teddy how it felt to pin down the mallard at 200 yards. He said he loved taking her down.

When we were kids we used to aim our unloaded rifles out the window and imagine what we could hit. We shared a bunk on the second floor. I remember the autumn months especially and the way our big elm tree turned from green to auburn. A slight tinge marking the advance of autumn. Other trees in the neighborhood had that same tinge of color. Birch. Ash. Maple. Cedar. Creeper. Dogwood. Elderberry. Fir. Hickory and Balsam. All the changes were there and could be felt and the birds we couldn't find were there nestled in their nest with surrounded by family.

Some weeks later when I returned from a hunt I sat myself by the living room window. I watched the last streaks of grey being inked out of the sky by the encroaching full moon. The storm that had played cat and mouse with me had not yet eased.

I remembered the conversation I had with my brother regarding my mom and dad:

"You still mad at mom, Teddy?"

"Sure, I am."

"What are you mad at?"

"I thought about that a lot and to be honest I can't quite pin it down. Sometimes I feel even guilty for thinking it. Like what did they do that was so bad? Maybe my own poor predicament has nothing to do with them, you know?"

"I hear what you're saying," I said. "I feel the same way too. It's like come on, dad, how could you be so foolish? Then I hear somebody saying to me: 'Hey, leave your old man alone. He's from another time and another place. Stop judging him. Stop making excuses for you own demise. Stop blaming your folks.' You know he had a point."

"Who's he?"

"Some guy in my head."

I switched on the little lamp overhead. The effort tired me and I slumped back onto the couch. It frightened me to be alone.

I sat in the glare of the new moon and breathed quietly. I seemed to be bruised just about everywhere, but apparently nothing was broken. I did not feel feverish but then this was just the weakness. I suspected it was more than exhaustion. I remembered a moment, as I had sat on that tree stand, when I had thought I was going to die; and I wondered whether I had inflicted on myself some permanent damage.

I checked my possessions too. My phone was still strapped to my belt and my wallet was neatly tucked in my coat pocket.

A moment of dizziness came and went. I opened the door of my bathroom and stood in front of the mirror. It was important not to permit myself the psychological attitudes of a beaten animal.

It turned out the Mum suffered a severe stroke and one of the extra hands named Warren found her on the floor Saturday morning. He had not heard her when she fell. When Mr. Smitty arrived at the hospital Mum was still awake and seemed to be conscious... but she could not speak. We later learned that it was a left brain stroke, the symptoms of which I won't go into for the time being. Later that day, she drifted into a coma, and never regained consciousness.

She died on Wednesday morning at 6am.

I have to admit I was a bit choked up when I heard. Here's the kicker: I'm not a proclaimed atheist but I don't believe in all that religious nonsense. The truth is I haven't had to deal with this kind of grief since the death of my only first cousin at the hands of a drunk driver over sixteen years ago. I've always been there to help counsel people in the church through these types of grief, but when it happens to your own family, it almost seems surreal. I keep wishing that all of this was just a bad dream, but I know it's not. It's like everything I ever learned about counseling has gone out the window. I do know the importance of grieving for yourself. After my mom died, at some point, I just couldn't feel God's presence with me.

Today when they buried the Mum, it reminded me of what I thought my mother should have had. I stared at her in casket, stroked her fine, thin hair, then stood back as they closed the casket lid. The pallbearers, all decked out in Sunday wear, hefted her up and led us down the lane. When I say should have had I mean with respects to time. My mother was not nearly old enough to be taken by such a ruthless disease. But death does not discriminate. And pain and heartache takes its share of the middle-aged.

At the time of my mother's death I was in debt over my head. My wife was pregnant with my first. I was the power of attorney and health care proxy for my mother who was disabled when she suffered a stroke that left her speech severely impaired and her right side mobility limited. She died soon after the stroke and I needed help paying the funeral expenses because Teddy refused. I had to bury my mother with no funeral. There was nothing I could do at the time. I was financially strapped with months of my mother in and out of the hospital. My mother did not have life insurance because both her and my dad could not afford it. The nursing home would have taken its proceeds, as is required by their policies, but it was only enough to cover the cremation expense. I had the ashes sealed in the urn just before I left for Brunswick. As far as I know my mother's still at the funeral home.

When my dad passed on, I was a lot better off so I had a tiny urn filled for my Mom and for my brother. I left myself out of it.

Some folks want part of themselves scattered in woods, or on bodies of water that have meaning to them. Personally, I don't worry about this nonsense of cremains being scattered. If God organized matter and created the universe in six days, why would anyone think he couldn't organize the remaining matter of a cremated deceased person for the purpose of resurrection.

When my Aunt May died twenty years ago she was cremated. My Uncle J insisted upon keeping her ashes on display in the dining room of the house that she loved and poured her heart and soul into a box that he purchased from the funeral home. Since then he has taken two girlfriends hardly on the same level as my mother on tours through her magnificent home. Both have something in mind, he romances them on my auntie's pension, yet refuses to bury her ashes. One of these women whom my Aunt intensely disliked because she was the town courtesan who hid behind her position as church secretary. She went through a bitter divorce and her daughter tried committing suicide four times. Still, my father, who is not the best judge of character, insists that she is "highly respected", or at least according to his lawyer friend who made my father his best friend while planning his estate. So here are my aunt's ashes on display in the dining room as Uncle J marches his girlfriends through her house. He wants to his cake and to eat it too.

I remember being ten or eleven years old. Having no place to call home. I was going from place to place but my Auntie would not hear of it. She took me in and made her home my home. She taught me so many things. Love and patience. How to grocery shop, cook and how to keep a clean and tidy home. Cleaning not my favourite. It made her happy so it made me happy. I would always get my chores finished after school. Because I so looked forward to our time together at the end of our long days. Her beauty shop was in our home. My Aunt May did all the neighbours hair not to mention my teachers. Which kept me on my best behaviour. Aunt May had many hobbies. One was sewing. She could make anything from bras to coats. With a purchase of a new sewing machine came lessons. She gave those lessons to me. She praised me for all I tried to make. But, I knew that I could never fill her shoes. Aunt May loved dogs. Her customers would buy her ceramic dogs. Even know I had to dust all of them. She had a collection from all over the world. I envied her great sense of humour. She was a very special person. She made life fun. We had good time together in our adult lives. She loved my girls.

My wife and I were talking on the phone one day about death and whether we wanted to be buried or cremated. She said she was afraid to be cremated because she doesn't want to feel the burning pain. I was sort of surprised she would even think that was possible. Was she under the mistaken belief that when you die you just sit around in your body, conscious and bored in your coffin? Trapped in you now lifeless shell?

I told my wife I wanted to be cremated so I didn't take up unnecessary space on some otherwise beautiful land.

Smitty's a devout Christian so I'm sure he stuck to the doctrine of the resurrection of the body.

Mum was buried in nearby Troy at the Mormon Pioneer Memorial Monument Cemetery. It's a private cemetery reserved for mostly rich Christians. Most of Smitty's family is there.

Smitty's Uncle Adams pipe-smoking grandfather is there. There are some other graves under the elm trees behind the fenced-in graves. Some are children. Elsie and Jimmy Wiggins, a brother and sister, died in Feb 1898 from smoke inhalation during a prairie fire. An infant of a neighbour named Joad Kramer was buried there, as was Joad's ten year old nephew named RJ.

The Smitty family have ties to the American Civil War and Mark Twain that date to the antebellum period when several large plantations owned the majority of the land in the Brunswick area. A descendant, Mrs. Jocelyn Kates kindly showed me her family cemetery. Located in her backyard the dozen stones date from the 1930s to the present. Two of the individuals were born in the 1870s, immediately after the Civil War, to parents who had been enslaved. Most of Jocelyn and Mum's great nieces and nephews are buried in this small family cemetery.

I was with my wife during the wake and funeral so I never really had a chance to think. Unlike my wife I hate funerals, I hate wakes. I hate group mourning. I hate the fact that we remember someone with a ceremony and a lot of talking about that person. Which is often by people who didn't know the person very well. Or if they did they don't talk about the true person. They talk about the idealized version. But we don't do more than that. It's an impersonal send off.

I hate the fact that I'm expected to go a long distance for a funeral which in its self is draining. What's worse is you drained both during the funerals and coming back so you're a shell of yourself for a couple of days until you return from the dead. I also find the idea that if I need to mourn, I need a ton of people I'm not close to around me to be absurd. I need to retreat and spend time truly grieving ie. Screaming, crying going thru the stages of grief, etc. Not with a bunch of people who are all trying to hold it together because we all can't make a scene. I think for me part of the problem is when you're at a service. You fall into what I call the big shocker. My Uncle Kendrick fell into this category back when his pops passed away. It's the hardest hit and the most numb. Your either go deep inside where you can't feel anything or your in so much pain your trying to hold yourself together from breaking down completely. And all the nice words and all the people who are offering support. Just makes you sick. You need to be alone so you can actually deal with it all. You want to tell everyone go jump or tell them where they can shove their condolences.

Aunt May dealt with the old man dying a little differently. Kinda like she was hit hard but didn't know how to deal with it. Too many trips to the punch bowl you know. You may be sad but your moving on and your mostly alright. So you feel weird this isn't hitting you very much. You stuck in a weird grief and guilt trip. Because while you feel bad you're not the person who having the most trouble. So you feel like you're not missing someone enough. So end up feeling worse.

I'm not feeling grief for Smitty. It's weird. I'm not hit much by grief realizing I may not have been as close to the person as some were. You feel guilty and out of place. As if you don't belong and you have no right to intrude on this service. You end up feeling horrible because you know you're not hurting like most everyone else. And there is nothing you can do to help.

When I look at Smitty I notice he isn't hit as hard as some of the others. Like Mrs. Smitty. Then Smitty's dealing with it his own way, right? Anybody's who's watching him and not convinced has to accept it. It's easy to be judgemental. But it's not fair. I can be horrible about picking up everyone's emotions and I can't take that right now.

I think I've been to four funerals my entire life. First, friends dad died suddenly, second, Great Uncle I never met, third, friends grandpa sick a long time, fourth grandmother who had been sick a long time, the last three were ok, sad but ok. I was mostly upset because of the pain they felt with their illnesses. The first was the worst, still hurts to this day. My friend's dad died of a heart attack, he was overweight but it's still tragic. My friend is one of the kindest people I have ever met. I think she's a turd but anyway her and I were close when we were younger and less so in high school. Her brother was on student council and so a lot of school people were at the funeral, and they didn't know her father. I know that it's a showing of support but when you don't know the person I think it's better not to go. It was also a terrible funeral, the reverend was someone else I have known my whole life and he was awful.

When I was a kid a lot of people went to the funeral to get out of school. I can't say I've ever let that one go, a memory complete with me watching a girl I dislike as she walked away from the teacher saying she was going to the funeral just to get out of the test like everyone else. Mind you there were some people who legit knew the family.

I also know someone who was very close to me whose uncle was murdered. He didn't invite me to the funeral but I'm not going to ask why. It's a person thing I was pretty distraught over it, though yes it didn't happen to me or my family. It is still a terrible situation with many sad repercussions. Anyway, I digress. Funerals and grief are very personal things. I generally say nothing and give people space offer my Hello if they need it but mostly stay away. It's a very personal thing.

I know people, particularly a co-worker, who makes it a point to go to every frisking funeral in this town" she's obsessed with it. I can't do that. I did go to another co-worker's father's funeral though that was three months after her mom passed away because I wanted to show her my support and that, even though I didn't know her Dad, I cared about her.

It happened when I was six years old. He was sixteen. It was a freak riding mower accident and the entire thing flipped over on top of him, crushing his lungs. He was dead before the paramedics arrived. It traumatized me greatly, and I hardly spoke an unnecessary word to anyone for the next eight years. Up until then, though, my family was extremely religious. Jehovah Witness, actually. My eldest sister and father are still religious to this day but after my brother's death my mother simply couldn't be bothered to care about anything, least of all showing up to church every Sunday. She stopped caring about everything, and her primary job was a al live-in caretaker for my well-off but in from grandparents. Her care for them grew lax and their health took a toll for it. It wasn't too long before their other son, my father's brother I assume, forced us out in the middle of the night, at gunpoint. I know what he did was far from legal, but my grandmother had died. She had many health issues and was bed ridden to her last days but my uncle decided it was my mother's deteriorating mental state that ultimately caused my grandmother's death.

12

Two Orange Man

Yesterday I heard snow geese flying over but the fog was so dense I never got a look at them, but it was good to hear them. After hearing the geese I did take a short drive into the countryside to see if any coyotes were around. I'd been mentally exhausted after the funeral and I needed some time alone. It's common to want to be alone after a death. When my grandfather died twenty years ago I didn't want to see anyone or talk to anyone. I put the answering machine on my phone and every night I would listen to messages and then delete them without calling anyone back. Every night before I went to bed, I would write how my day was and how I was feeling. I kept a journal. I still like to think of grieving like walking along the seashore. You walk along, all is calm and the small waves are rolling gently over your feet. Then all of a sudden a big wave comes crashing in and sends you flying. It will affect you physically, emotionally, spiritually. I'm not hit too hard from the Mum dying but I feel for Mr. Smitty. Mr. Smitty's a lot like my Teddy in many ways and I suspect he might react the same way my brother had with my own mother's death. I'm guessing.

It began when my mother complained of pain in her rib cage for some weeks before she finally saw a doctor. The tumor that the subsequent X-rays discovered in my mother's left lung was the size of a softball, a giant dark circle in the light area of my mother's lung in the X-Ray photos, and emergency surgery was immediately scheduled to remove the entire lung and tumor inside it. Subsequent tests, however, showed that the cancer had spread from the lung into my mom's liver, bones, and lymph node system. The cancer was at "Stage Four" and removing the tumor would not help; the cancer had already spread. The doctors privately told me there was no hope, that my mother might last four more months. My brother was in San Francisco at the time, besides my mother, it was just Shirley (my girlfriend at the time) and I in that grim hospital room on that dreadful day when test after test came back with the worst possible results.

My mother cried and cried and made many phone calls. By the end of the day, however, she had stopped crying; she seemed exhausted, and she simply wanted to go home. The sense of haste and emergency of the previous days was gone; there was nothing modern medicine could do for my mother, and the hospital released her. The chemotherapy would start the next week. I wheeled her out of the hospital exit in a wheelchair as we waited for Shirley to swing the car around front. It was dark out by then. The scene was surreal. It seemed like a movie; this kind of day only occurred in movies. We did not talk. We were numb. The calm after the storm.

Earlier that day my father and I finally had gotten a moment away from my mom in the hospital cafeteria and he had cried like a baby with his face in his hands. I put my arm around him, oblivious to all the stares of everyone else in the cafeteria at us. My world was crumbling, with my father's illness, but my mother's entire universe was falling utterly to pieces right in front of her, with her husband threatened. I was torn between being strong for my mother and feeling my own grief. "I am the oldest child; it is my job to be strong; and I cannot fall apart myself. What would Teddy think if the oldest fell apart? If my mother were incapacitated, it is my job to lead." So I thought at the time. And so I acted for more than a year.

My father survived for another four months, although the doctors gave him only two. I always admired my father for proving those horrible doctors wrong. He deteriorated slowly but certainly, the chemotherapy slowing but not stopping the spread of the cancer. Finally, the alienating march of the tumors reached the brain and a small army of tiny tumors depressed vital parts of the brain dealing with breathing and heartbeat and my father finally died.

I have never seen anything as beautiful and touching as my father caring for my mother as she retreated into a sort of second infancy. First, she lost the capacity to speak and think clearly. Then my mom could no longer walk without help, and finally she could not walk at all. By the end she had shriveled up, could recognize nobody, and had to be washed an fed as if she were a baby. My father would wake up in the morning and wash her body. Although she could not recognize anyone, my father would talk to her lovingly as he brushed her hair:

"Good morning, my darling! You look so beautiful today!"

He brushed her teeth. He changed her diapers. This was marriage: "until death do us part." It was the strangest thing I'd ever seen.

13
The Stomach Of A Clarinet

Christmas came and went. Our weather turned bitter cold. Alfred and I turned over the New Year with the purchase of a new tractor. Dora's eldest daughter got engaged and Franklin, the Doyle's kid, turned the big 40. Lucky him.

When I asked my twin how he was progressing, he mentioned he was having some difficulty. When I asked Teddy to elaborate without sounding too quirky he said he was having trust issues with his wife. He asked me in all my years of marriage if I'd ever suspected Shelley of cheating. I told him no. He went on asking me other questions that were all in some way variant of the first and after the fifth question I asked him to stop. I went on further saying that infidelity wasn't an option and if he was certain then he should let her go.

"No second chances?"

"No second chances," I said and I followed up with a number of probing questions that included the following:

"Did you see your wife with another man?"

"No."

"Has anyone been calling the house and hanging up?"

"No."

"Any strange credit card entries?"

"No."

"There must have been something that sparked your fear. Are you cheating?"

Then came thunder. And lightning.

The thunder was the realization that my brother was in fact cheating on his wife. And now he was dealing with his conscious (that's lightning).

"Who is she?"

"Nobody."

"She has to be somebody," I said. "Do you love her?"

"Yes."

"Are you planning on leaving your wife?"

"No."

I remember feeling both relieved and saddened by the news. On one hand, I wanted his family to remain together but on the other I wanted him to be loved.

"What do you plan to do?"

"Nothing."

"Nothing?"

"She's married."

"Your mistress is married?"

It was then that Teddy became angered and asked me not to refer to Laila as a "mistress." So I didn't.

The other thing my brother mentioned was that he had contemplated suicide.

I was perfectly annoyed when I heard him say that, and I told him if he was really serious about suicide he ought to jump off a bridge. "This way you wouldn't have to worry."

"Worry about what?"

"Failing." I added, "Just be sure you're over concrete."

"That would be an awful way to go."

"Not to worry. You'd probably pass out before impact."

"Is that all you have to say?"

"Yes," I said.

The last I heard Teddy had checked into a psyche ward. I was pleased to hear that he was somewhere safe. Help him to relax. Sleep. Quit smoking. Give up booze and dope. Leave anxiety at bay. The anchor of restlessness. That restlessness will weight you down.

The old boy came through in the long run and the last I heard he was out of the ward and working again. He'd paid a visit to Laila and broke the affair. Patched things up with Trudy and consolidated his debt, something about carrying a hundred year annuity.

Sometime around the end of March while I was preparing for Easter Teddy sent me a postcard from California. Crazy son-of-a-gun! It read:

"I'm saved. God Bless Bank of America. I can live again.
 Art of the deal real estate, Donald trump over Mother Theresa
  Business window cleaning ran out when he paid us
  Lied in the interview lied to customers lied to boss
  Business invention went sour
  Got married and got my first credit card
  Travelled the world and got my second credit card
  Bought my first home on my third credit card

> *Bought my first car with my fourth credit card*
> *Got a job got a kid got another kid kept up with payments with a fifth credit card*
> *Lost my job and refinanced the house*
> *Got another job, opened up a part time business*
> *Got a sixth credit card to meet payments*
> *Contemplated divorce, handcuffed the wife and kids and left for the desert where they don't speak the time, driving a rig*
> *God Bless Bank of America I'm indebted to you for life."*
> Love, Teddy

The rest of us here in Brunswick continued on with the same old, same old which is how I prefer it. My Becky got braces. Charlotte scored a First Place in Public Speaking commemorating her passion for young women's liberation – GOOD for her! Shelley heard from her sister and made plans with her cousins for the summer – again WHOOPEE! Me? I got a brand new 65" HD TV with a satellite dish from the Smitty's. Must have been a congratulatory award. It's alright. I guess I've gotten greedy in my middle age. I really shouldn't complain. Just last week Mrs. Smitty signed me up for a Pension Plan that included the rest of the family. My girls are guaranteed to retire by the age of 40 with a trust fund aimed to pay for university. My wife doesn't have to work after she turns 50. That's not so bad considering we were broke only fifteen years ago. Me? I'm already retired as far as I'm concerned. I have a scheduled lunch with Mrs. Smitty and some of the hired hands later today. On Friday some of us are headed to the Old Burrow's Farm where its being converted to a urine replenishing facility. Next month its Lyle Cobalt's Farm. He's going into water too. In the meantime, I've got livestock to tend do. Miss Bessie is expecting.

Then there's enough around the farm to keep me busy. The word out is Alfred got wise ever since Mum's passing and dug up some of his wealth from under his mattress and invested in Homer's water business. The story goes he'd gotten some heck from the old lady until the first residual cheque came in for fifteen thousand bucks.

Josephine broke any rumours of an engagement with Clifford by changing her phone number. Henry left for India investing in a power plant and Sarah Ann made a vow never to get married.

George Barnwell came back into town and tried hustling Mrs. Smitty into converting the farm into a fifty-storey condominium. She had both Frodo and Pooches make spaghetti out of his shoe laces.

Lastly, with Mum out of the picture, it's been my responsibility that the other hands remain respectful in this time of psychological torture. As is often the case with Death and Natural Wealth Selection when much of the talk revolves slitting an inheritance into three halves.

You are invited to a preview of

SUPEREGO MAN

SUPEREGO MAN is an invitingly creepy tale involving a fun-loving, irresponsible father of four boys. Poor Ed is having a hard time keeping a job and an overbearing wife from taking a hatchet to his throat.

CHAPTER ONE

In the interest of being perfectly honest I must share with you a few personal things about myself before we begin. I'm an inch shy of six feet and I weigh one hundred and sixty pounds. My goal is to weigh one hundred and fifty pounds by the end of the month. I'm confident I can do it as long as I stay off the Junior Chickens. I'm not big on video games but I like surfing on the net. I gotta be careful because last month I ran up the net bill sky high and Monica, my wife, grounded me for a week. No TV or computer, she said. I know it sounds ridiculous for a grown man but as long as I'm on government disability she's the boss.

    I have four wonderful kids, all boys. Dakota is thirteen and the eldest of four boys so he's heard enough cussing between me and Monica to last a lifetime. One time his mom threw a toaster clear across the kitchen table smacking yours truly square on the forehead. I didn't say a word and I told Dakota in private that I deserved that three inch gash above my right eye since I neglected to pay the phone bill. I squandered the money on some girlie books and when the time came to pay I didn't have enough money so I left it until a creditor got a hold of it and when the phone started ringing at five o'clock in the morning I knew I couldn't hide it from the missus any longer.

    "I pushed it too far, Sport," I told my son. "I got a little careless. I got to be more on the ball next time."

I've always shared my true feelings to Dakota and I think he resents me for that. He told me once he didn't mind talking table tennis (our favourite sport) or game hunting or even the value of a good education but he hated when I talked about his mom. Especially on the subject of money.

"Money represents a lot of bad things for me," he told me once, "mom's constant uneasiness about getting a bigger house, your failure to find a decent paying job. You say the hell with this creditor and the hell with that creditor and you wonder why mom gets in on it and shoves it back in your face. Well, you can't say eff to this creditor or eff to that creditor. They eff you this way and they crap on you that way when you don't return their phone calls, then you really learn who is effed when you're credit rating goes to crap! I really hate money with a passion. Hate it! Hate it! Super hate it!"

Wow! I didn't realize my son was so angry. I know I haven't been perfect but I've done my best. It's a good thing he has his brothers.

Tyler's my youngest. He loves to read. His favourite book is Charlotte's Web. He's a lot like Wilbur. He's very fragile. Tyler's the munch-kin. He's only eight. He shares the same facial qualities as Dakota: a pointed face with blue eyes and blond hair curling over his shoulders. There's Zachariah. He likes Zach. He's nine and really strong for his age. He's also impossible to beat in chess. Ryan is ten and the smartest of the four, which he always sees as a disadvantage. I don't. I wish I could finish a Rubik's cube in twenty nine seconds like he can. I think Ryan can be a doctor if he applies himself. Not like Dakota. I'm sorry to say but my first-born isn't up to par mentally. The only thing he's got going is he's grown six inches in the last six months. The girls like him. I can tell cause I catch them staring at him anytime I pick him up from school. I don't know what made Dakota grow so tall. Maybe it's all the raw broccoli. He loves raw broccoli and eats a whole bunch almost every other day.

Anyway, as I was eluding to between the wife and I, Dakota and his brothers like to sneak away when all the cussing between the wife and I starts. They scoot off to the basement of our two-storey and perch themselves in the furnace room where it's super dark and toasty warm in the winter months and there with a tiny flashlight and four couch cushions set up camp. There's a little nest in the furnace room which is the under path of our basement stairs. I heard them play a game called V-Combat Warfare. They act as soldiers. The place under the stairs is the Bunker. The Bunker is where they plan their mission. Each week they take their turns and contribute a different assignment. They've designed routes, maps and stations corresponding with the rest of the rooms of our house to resemble real combat zones of warfare. For example: They use the basement couches as our sleeping quarters; the kitchen as the Mess Hall. The washrooms are enemy camps. Closets are prisoner's cells. The basement is the valley, the main floor the jungle and the second floor to the house is the mountain. Monica and I have talked about these routes and given the boys the okay throughout the entire house excluding my den. My den is located on the far side of the basement next to the laundry room. It's away from the stairs so they're not tempted to enter so much. I've hung a sign on the den's door that reads KEEP OUT – UNDER NO CURCUMSTANCES ARE YOU OR ANYONE

ALLOWED IN THE DEN. TRESSPASSERS WILL BE SHOT!

A lot of paranormal things have happened in my den where I write so I like to keep it locked. None of it has been particularly violent but chairs have moved up in the air about backwards and frontwards then slammed on the ground. Doorknobs twist and my IPAD was taken. I found it one morning after it randomly disappeared, left my room for two minutes, came back and it was gone. Recently I came into my den and found writing on one of my whiteboards that I found very strange. I love my den but Dakota made the mistake of entering it not too long ago and the next thing you know he's covered in a pool of blood. I rushed him to the hospital and had him stitched up with a doctor, Dr. Kailan, who told me Dakota needed twelve stitches on his left hand.

I remember describing to Dr. K that I thought the knife incident was an accident and that the blade must have slipped in my son's hand.

"You keep your knives in your den, do you?" Doctor K asked me.

"I keep my knives and guns in a locked cabinet."

"I see."

"I have the only key. I must have accidentally left it unlocked."

"You must have."

It's been months since the accident. I don't think I'll ever understand how I left the cabinet unlocked. Anyway, no real harm done. Dakota survived. Although, I will tell you Tyler is madder than hell. Any chance he gets he reminds me of the ghost in my den. I listen to him but I don't pay much attention.

What else? Last year Tyler was asked to join Cubs and quit after the first week. He hated it. Too many of the kids wanted to tie rope and fish. He wanted to play video games. Did I mention my Ryan hogs the TV and he's always saying he wants to commit suicide. He blames Monica and me. Monica mostly. He says she's always giving him heck when she should be giving me heck. I don't think he's being fair. Just last week I was sick with strep and Monica pulled me and the kids around town when it was raining and drove me batty. One of the places we went was the bookstore and Monica bought three books (all self-help) with my money I saved. Zach said I stole it from him but eff him cause I really saved it. I told Monica that my money was mine and I could do whatever I want with it. My wife said she would pay me back. That still isn't fair, but oh well. She won't remember to pay me back. So then we went to Starbucks and my throat was freaking hurting horribly. I didn't see anything I wanted at Starbucks so I told her I didn't want anything. She ordered me ice coffee and expected me to drink it. I hate coffee. I told her I didn't want it and she freaked out. I did so much more stuff, and when the day was over, we went home.

I'll tell you another thing about my wife and how mean she gets if you don't do what she wants when she wants. I remember one time I forgot to put the pancake syrup back in the fridge and she stormed into the kitchen found the syrup bottle on the sink and demanded that I drop everything I was doing and put it back where it belonged. Guess what? She called me a little bastard and threw the bottle at me just as I was shutting off my computer! That was like five or six weeks ago when I was like almost finished the first draft to my children's novel.

And also, she's a bully and pushes my kids around and she always makes them cry. Oh yeah, did I mention she's bipolar? Starting last winter she started having manic episodes at night. She would yell at me and Tyler and sometimes Zach and run away. Dakota and I tried to stop her but she got out and it was freezing cold and she wouldn't bring a coat and would stumble around the street and then hide when we tried to go and get her. So many times we found her in a coffee shop passed out from taking too many pills. This happened like every other month and when these episodes did occur she would act like it didn't happen. The last time she disappeared for a night saying she needed time alone in a motel. It's all very sick I think. Ryan refuses to believe that anything is wrong with her even though it's been months since we've sat down at the same table for supper. We've pushed her to go see a psychiatrist, but she lies to us and tells us that she has when we know that she hasn't. My youngest is at the end of his ropes and I feel like I have run out of options to help her. I'm convinced that she's suffering from Bipolar.

Dakota's not too keen on this mental stuff and thinks she's possessed by the devil and that some demon is influencing her. I don't know if he's stupid or lying to me, it's hard to tell cause he's a really good liar. Not too long ago my wife threw a big hissy fit saying that I'm always in her room and that I always leave it a mess. So she goes on and says more and more stupid crap saying I'm stupid and that no one will ever take me seriously, again she's talking about stupid crap. Then she says she wants me to clean her room every Saturday morning (we have separate rooms) and I'm like OK but what about her sons. I cleaned her room and stuff and when I tried talking to her she totally bailed on me. So I told Ryan (big mistake!) and Monica found out and she threw another hissy fit again saying oh that I can't be trusted. I had a face to face with her and she says no bleeping way! I'm like you're not giving me a chance. Then I'm super mad and I totally rant out my feelings in front of my boys who say nothing cause I think they're just used to it. Then my youngest goes and tells my wife everything I said including when I said I hated her. I'm like what are you saying dude?!

Monica eventually confronts me and says "why the eff are you saying you hate me?!"

I'm like I didn't mean it I was just mad. I go to my room now and when she gets off work.

...

www.ingramcontent.com/pod-product-compliance
Lightning Source LLC
Chambersburg PA
CBHW030654220526
45463CB00005B/1772